AF599080

MIDSTREAM

MID STREAM

A LIFE REMADE IN 50 SWIMS

KATE WASHINGTON

Beacon Press
BOSTON

BEACON PRESS
24 Farnsworth Street
Boston, Massachusetts
www.beacon.org

Beacon Press books
are published under the auspices of
the Unitarian Universalist Association of Congregations.

Printed in the United States of America

29 28 27 26 8 7 6 5 4 3 2 1

This book is printed on acid-free paper that meets the uncoated paper
ANSI/NISO specifications for permanence as revised in 1992.

Text design and composition by Kim Arney

*Library of Congress Cataloguing-in-Publication
Data is available for this title.*
Hardcover ISBN: 978-0-8070-2354-9
E-book ISBN: 978-0-8070-2355-6
Audiobook: 978-0-8070-2457-7

The authorized representative in the EU for product safety
and compliance is Easy Access System Europe 16879218, Mustamäe tee 50,
10621 Tallinn, Estonia: https://beacon.org/eu-contact.

For Nora and Lucy,
with all my love and my
top two pieces of maternal advice:
Never forget what brings you joy,
and always pack a swimsuit.

CONTENTS

INTRODUCTION

TAKING THE WATERS

DUNK 1: *Pacific Ocean*

Anchorless, my body floated free, jolted by cold as the surf tossed me back and forth. As I struggled to my feet in shifting sand, choppy waves lapping my calves, a fizzy hot chill crept up my legs and turned my skin a blotchy coral. I whooped and lay back down in the water before I could lose my nerve. It was April 2021, a day of stiff winds on the northern California coast. I'd just been vaccinated for COVID-19, and in those first weeks of hopeful postshot socializing, friends had invited me on a day trip to eat oysters in the sunshine near Point Reyes. I asked if we could make a detour to nearby Dillon Beach for a cold plunge. We had to run far down the wide, flat sands to get deep enough to go all the way under the shallow surf. Three immersions later, I waded back out knotty haired, salt stinging my eyes and nose, exhilarated, every sense tingling, alive. For a moment, water, wind, sand, and sun washed away the doldrums of the pandemic and the years of caretaking, family obligation, and burnout that for me had preceded it.

That brief dip in the turbulent Pacific was the first of fifty such expeditions I had planned. I was forty-eight-and-a-half years old that day—I add the half with the exactness my kid self would have insisted on—and my life felt constrained and constraining, dull and joyless, full of doing for others while neglecting myself. Although my next milestone birthday was a year and a half away, I could see it on the horizon, looming. Was I really going to turn fifty feeling stuck and depleted? Was this all the middle of my life had to offer? What could I do to mark a new decade that wouldn't punish myself, like so many such goals (weight loss, say), but might actually be a fun quest?

That's how I hatched the idea for what I came to call the 50 Dunks Project. My plan was to get in fifty different natural bodies of water before turning fifty in October 2022. Swimming holes, hot springs, rivers, lakes, tiny creeks, and oceans all counted. I could swim, soak, dive, duck under, or jump into the middle of the current, so long as I went all the way under. However I got in the water, I hoped it might dissolve my midlife stagnation.

~~~

In one of the many photo albums my mother painstakingly assembled, there's a faded picture of my dad holding me in a creek with a bluff behind us, me in pigtails and a candy-striped swimsuit, both of us soaked and grinning. I was maybe seven or eight years old, and we were camping in the geologic no-man's-land where the Sierra Nevada gives way to the Cascade Range. I had been perched on the overhanging bank above the swift, deep creek, hesitating over whether to jump, when my
~~~

dad settled the question with a shove. I sank to the soft creek bed and popped up spluttering and laughing. My mom was furious. She never forgave my dad, but I did; the shock of the cold was fun.

I've loved the water since childhood. A creek, dammed to form a freshwater swimming pool, runs through my hometown of Chico, California, and on hundred-degree days we trudged down dusty trails, scented with feral blackberries, to splash there. At my Episcopalian church camp, they rented a U-Haul (really) to transport us kids to beach days at teeth-chattering Lake Tahoe; I always swam, even in June when the water was coldest. After my parents put in a pool, my brother and I spent long blazing afternoons racing underwater holding our breath, no adult in sight. Summer after summer, I swam so much, my feet dried and cracked from chlorine.

Nevertheless, I was a bookish kid who thought of herself as unathletic. I was slow and stocky, and the sports then popular for girls—soccer, tennis, volleyball—valued speed and agility over strength. Playing soccer, I was stuck on defense while our coach screamed "Hustle!" That began my embrace of my intellectual self and the abandonment of my physical side. In the water, strength and extra body fat could have been advantages, but the youth swim team was too expensive and too much hassle for my parents. By high school I was too intimidated to join a team full of longtime competitors. Now, I wonder if a grueling team experience would have killed my enjoyment of the water, or if I would have found a love for and connection with my body and athleticism that I abandoned too young. Back then, it wasn't that deep; I just couldn't stomach making a fool out of myself by being bad at something.

My striving, perfectionist side always coexisted uneasily with '70s free-range kid life. Sure, I wanted to spend whole afternoons falling backward with a splash, just like in the old ad urging me to "take the Nestea plunge," but I also wanted all the gold stars I could garner. When my fifth-grade teacher offered an extra star on the class book-report chart for each one hundred pages read, I raided my parents' shelves for so many fat, age-inappropriate Judith Krantz paperbacks that the teacher had to tape up extra poster boards. I had other reasons for retreating with books. My parents' relationship was volatile, and my mother was bipolar and often depressed. I learned early to read a room's emotional temperature, fend for myself, and try to be no trouble.

To say that I rushed into adulthood would be an understatement. By high school, I wanted out of my hometown. Straight As came easily, and I went to the East Coast for college. I spent summers not splashing in creeks but suffering through wearing pantyhose to internships in muggy DC. My ambition, however, had little direction. By senior year, I didn't know what to do with myself after graduation, so I applied to graduate school. Now I wish that I had spent my early twenties traveling on a shoestring, dancing, sleeping with unsuitable men, and dabbling in the occasional illicit drugs. Instead, I started a PhD program at age twenty-one. I thought I wanted to become a professor and lead the life of the mind, but really, I feared the unknown. The one thing I knew was that I wanted to go home, so I applied only to schools in the West. I squeaked into Stanford's English department off the waiting list, and in 1996 that's where I met Brad, who became my husband. He and I married in 1999, and I finished my dissertation three months later. I was twenty-six. I left academia to pursue writing and editing jobs; in 2002, Brad took a tenure-track job at Sacramento State University. We had two daughters, Nora in 2005 and Lucy in 2009.

I never saw the downsides of conventional grown-up life coming until the complicated griefs and gender inequities of adulthood smacked me in the face. In 2010, when the girls were four years old and six months, my mother died by suicide, leaving me reeling. A few months later, when I was still dazed with grief, Brad took on a demanding new role as his department's chair. That shifted almost all childcare and household responsibilities onto me, just when they had ballooned with a new baby. I didn't realize how abandoned I felt until later, but it created a rift in our marriage. That rift only worsened after another catastrophe: Brad's extended treatment for aggressive lymphoma, with which he was diagnosed in 2015. In 2016, he needed a stem cell transplant to save his life; the complications nearly killed him, and he was hospitalized for more than four months. As his caregiver, I was beyond overwhelmed—so much so that I wrote a book about it. Titled *Already Toast: Caregiving and Burnout in America*, it was published in March 2021, less than a month before that April dunk in the Pacific.

With that professional success, I felt like I ought to have been happy, but instead I was burned out, emotionally and creatively drained. My misery came right on schedule. Studies have shown that, for most people, happiness dips to its nadir in the late forties. Not coincidentally, that's also the average age of the American caregiver. Women endure additional unpleasantness at the nadir: many, me included, struggle with perimenopause, including hormonal shifts that spark rage, sapping the estrogen that kept us content through mothering and caretaking. No wonder I wasn't enjoying getting older. I'd poured out everything for others, while doing little for myself and getting less care in return. Somewhere amid caregiving, raising our daughters, running a household, and trying to juggle all that with some semblance of a writing career, I'd lost touch with both myself and my husband.

Brad's cancer changed us both, in different ways. I recently heard Maggie Smith, the poet, on Lyz Lenz's podcast *This American Ex-Wife* (which takes its name from her bestselling 2024 book), speaking of people who marry in their twenties as "amorphous beings." When you marry young, you grow up in the marriage; often, she said, "the tendrils of that plant snake in opposite directions." Our tendrils were diverging well before Brad was sick, with separate interests and the pull of careers, but afterward it was like we were strangers. By the pandemic, we had been living as roommates for years. Brad remained immune compromised long post-transplant, and the unknown virus thrust us back into a caregiving dynamic. Then came the month of smoke. In a stifling August 2020 heat wave, eerie dry thunderstorms ignited lightning fires up and down northern California. The skies clouded, the sun turned red, and flakes of ash grayed my backyard. Once, desperate for exercise despite hazardous air quality, I tried to swim backstroke wearing an N95 mask; it was not a success. The torpor of those days stayed with me. Over my 50 Dunks Project, whenever I was tempted to bail on an expedition, I remembered that imprisonment, a reminder to get out while the getting was good.

~~~
~~~

A lifelong Californian, I never lose my sense of wonder at seeing deep cold rivers snaking through bone-dry hills, and little brings me more pleasure than swimming in them. In an arid country, water is magic. As Bonnie Tsui writes in *Why We Swim*, "There is a seductiveness to water. From afar, it gleams and glistens, a shiny liquid jewel. . . . It swirls, fans, and coalesces, embracing you. It holds you and yet cannot be held by you. When we immerse ourselves, something is awakened."

I feel that awakening every time I swim. It's not easy for me—a classic older-daughter planner and overthinker—to get out of my head and into the moment, but floating on my back, splashing my kids, diving to fetch rocks, or turning somersaults does it. Let me be clear: I get in the water for fun, not ambitious exercise, and my expeditions were the mildest of adventures, not feats of endurance or athleticism. I quit doing laps when the dull back-and-forth started to suck the joy out of water. I want to swim like I did as a kid, not like Katie Ledecky.

I took on my goal of fifty swims almost lightly, as an antidote to the long seclusion of the pandemic and a way to bring some fun and play into my responsibility-bound midlife. Some part of me, though, knew I had to coax myself out of melancholy, like an ailing Victorian lady sending myself to the seaside to take the waters. I think often of a well-known exchange from an Isak Dinesen story, in which one character offers "a cure for everything: salt water." Salt water, the other asks? "'Yes,' he said. "In one way or the other. Sweat, or tears, or the salt sea.'" I didn't know it at the time, but my chilly April dip into the saline Pacific began to cure my self-alienation. I was still the cautious kid who hesitated to jump in midstream, but on that day, I gave myself the push I needed.

CHAPTER ONE

A SPRING-FED STREAM

DUNK 5: *Jones Creek*
DUNK 6: *Butte Creek*

"You're tailgating," Brad said. My face turned hot.

"I'm totally boxed in," I said. "I'm trying to stay back, but this guy is right on my ass." I was driving on a winding two-lane highway full of blind curves and double yellow lines. As often happened on this route to our shared family cabin in the mountains, the slow driver ahead refused to pull into a turnout so drivers behind him could pass.

"Would you just slow down?" he continued.

"Like I said, I'm trying." My tone turned clipped, my temper accelerating as fast as the guy behind me when I tapped my brakes.

It was Father's Day of 2021, and Brad, our two daughters—then fifteen and eleven—and I were headed to the tiny mountain community of Jonesville, California, a collection of ramshackle summer cabins at the northern tip of Butte County. We were running late for lunch with my dad and my brother's family. It had been a hectic few weeks in the rush to the last day of school, and I was tired going into the day trip, a two-and-a-half-hour drive from our home in Sacramento. For years, we had gone to the cabin for overnights and long weekends. I wanted to spend the night on this weekend as well, but we were squeezing the trip in between Lucy's softball practices for an upcoming tournament and other obligations. Our trips to the cabin had dwindled. When the girls were younger, and before Brad got sick, we had more time to relax there, even though conditions might best be described as rustic. Now, however, it was often uncomfortable for Brad to stay long, given his chronic illness, and the girls were busier with activities. If we went for a trip longer than a night or two, it was usually me and the kids, one small sign of all the ways our family was splintering.

I was annoyed well before we got to the point of winding roads and tailgaters. It was the hottest day of the year so far, one hundred degrees before noon, and it had been a frazzled scramble to get out the door. I drove with lists of all I had to do, for that day and the week ahead, running through my mind. We were almost to the small town of Live Oak, a little less than an hour north of Sacramento, when I broke the silence.

"Hey," I said, "I've been thinking. I do pretty much all the cooking and planning. We need to divide it up more this summer. I need each of the three of you to take one dinner a week to be responsible for." Brad and I had agreed on a simple division of labor when we first moved in together: I would cook, he would clean up. Back then, it seemed equitable, but over time, I realized it wasn't. Feeding a family of four required a mountain of invisible mental labor beneath the small visible summit of actual dinners, but cleaning up was just cleaning up. He'd agreed to take one night a week of dinner, and he made sloppy joes and a limited other repertoire regularly, but my efforts to push him into more than that had failed. It seemed easier to force our daughters to do more than to keep cajoling my husband.

Both girls moaned. "What are we supposed to make?" said Lucy.

"Look, it doesn't have to be fancy," I said. "Make grilled cheese sandwiches for all I care. But I need more of a break."

"Maybe we should have talked about this before you sprang it on the girls," said Brad. He had a point—parenting decisions shouldn't be unilateral—but our many conversations about reducing my household load had never produced lasting results.

"I'm sick of asking for help and not getting it," I said. "Now I'm telling you all. You two are old enough to contribute more."

"But it's not fair!" the kids chorused.

"If it's unfair to anyone, it's me," I said. "I'll still be doing four nights a week and each of you will be doing one. How is that unfair?"

My question met stony silence as I pulled into the parking lot of El Bajio, a big Mexican market that made excellent ceviche and guacamole. Across the highway was a roadside stand selling grilled chickens, then ten dollars each. Our whole extended family loved them, and I had offered to pick up appetizers and chickens for our family lunch.

I can't remember if I asked Brad and the kids to do half the errand and they refused, or if I, martyr-like, took it all on myself. I do know I left the air-conditioning running for them while they sat in the car and I hustled to and fro over hot asphalt, fetching everything.

"Tres pollos, por favor," I said to the man who sold the chicken.

"*Tres pollitos, sí,*" he replied. His heavy cleaver thwacked through the bones, the fatty scent of charred chicken skin hit my nostrils, and I half wished for a cleaver of my own. I wanted to hit something, anything, with that kind of force.

"Salsa? Tortillas?" he asked. *Sí* and *sí*, I nodded.

I returned to the car, arms full of lunch for ten people.

"That took a while," Brad said.

"It would have been quicker if any of you had helped."

More tense silence lasted until Brad commented on the tailgating. In those days I came to every interaction with him exasperated and primed for a fight, and that's what we had, even though the girls were in the back seat. I couldn't let anything go, so when he continued to tell me to slow down, I exploded.

"Look, do you want to drive?"

"Not especially," he said. "I just want you to drive safely."

"I'm doing fucking everything here and I'm driving perfectly safely," I yelled back.

"It's not safe for you to drive when you're upset," he said, raising his voice in turn.

"If you stop fucking criticizing me, I won't be upset."

We went on and on, a tedious recapitulation of every dumb fight we'd ever had, until I spotted a turnout and screeched into it.

"Fine," I spat out. "You fucking drive for a change."

I flung open the car door, wrenched my whole body to slam it shut, and threw my key chain to the ground. The key fob popped apart, and my jaw clenched with shame as I scoured the pine needles and roadside detritus for tiny pieces of plastic. I hated acting like this—the way my mom raged when I was a kid—but I couldn't stop my tantrum. After decades of marriage and years of intense caretaking, I was as dry and crisp and ready to burn as the mountain landscape we were driving through.

~~~

I brought an infinite number of resentments, fresh and ancient, small and big, to that fight about nothing important, and I'm still tempted to detail every one of them. It's so easy for me to slip into that mode, into the patterns that several couples counselors warned us against. How he always did this or never did that or how lonely and unsupported I felt. But here's the deeper truth: it was never a matter of who was right and who was wrong. It didn't matter if I was tailgating. What mattered was that we had lost the love and appreciation we'd had for each other. We approached each other without curiosity, care, or empathy. We had never spoken the same emotional language, and by then we couldn't communicate about anything, even the smallest disagreement, without me blaming and him stonewalling.

When Brad and I met in graduate school, I was lonely, depressed, and hungry for any kind of love. I was too insecure to enjoy teaching students almost my own age, and my specialty—Victorian literature—was low prestige in my program's unspoken pecking order, below such "good" fields as eighteenth-century literature and modernism. My department embodied the tyranny of petty difference; I learned almost as much about the politics of academia as about the Brontës. Brad entered the program as a first-year PhD student when I was in my second year, but he was older than I, having already earned a master's degree in his native Canada. We met at a party,
~~~

bantering about obscure '80s bands; he called to ask me out a couple of days later. Our shared familiarity with the Mighty Lemon Drops seemed as good a common ground as any, and a few dates turned us into a couple. I liked his dry humor, and he was kind and loving; plus, he was just about the only cute, single straight man to be found in a graduate program in English. Shuffles in roommates and apartments led us to move in together just ten months later. Palo Alto was in the first wave of the dot-com boom, and the rental market was hostile to graduate students on a $12,000-per-year stipend.

In domesticity, as in everything, I wanted to earn a gold star. I went to IKEA and set up our hobbit-like cottage with a dining table, cheap (but framed) art, and fluffy towels that mildewed in its winter dampness. I invited friends over for dinner parties I planned earnestly from *Cook's Illustrated* and *The New Basics* and *The Cake Bible*, and, per our agreement, he did the dishes. Cooking doubled as a hobby and a necessity, and eating with friends was entertainment we could afford. I paired cheap Trader Joe's wine with the meals and teased Brad about the unholy Kool-Aid concoctions that he preferred, but behind my teasing lay both secret embarrassment and, in truth, the seeds of disdain. We had plenty of differences: I wanted those towels folded the way my mom did it; he didn't care. He wanted to leave papers and books in towering stacks in our minuscule shared office space; I was driven crazy by clutter. We fought, and I yelled, but to me that was normal. We were babies playing at being grown-ups.

When I was twenty-six, I felt like it was about time we got married. He didn't; I pressed. I should have taken a hint from his reluctance, but I was thirsty for security, and I had never seen a functional romantic relationship up close. I didn't know what to look for in a pairing that could go the distance, so a simulacrum of partnership and the adult stability that marriage promised were good enough for me. I was too insecure to know myself or realize it might be a bad sign that we didn't like to do the same things. He never enjoyed water or swimming—a childhood viewing of *Jaws* had left him with an unshakable shark phobia—and he could take or leave the outdoors, though he made valiant (if brief) efforts to enjoy camping and hiking for my sake. I didn't care about golf, abstruse philosophical debates with other grad students, or the sports fandom he was obsessed with, aside from a fondness for the San Francisco Giants. We found common ground listening to baseball games on the radio and driving over to the coast for beach picnics, though I never went into the ocean; it was too rough.

Although we seemed intellectually compatible, what with both being PhD students in English, we were at opposite ends of that departmental pecking order. Brad was a golden boy, a star modernist student of a star professor who never liked me. He also was, and remains, a true academic, absorbed by the life of the mind. I didn't have the patience or deep interest for yearslong academic projects, and by my fourth year, midway through my dissertation, I was sure I wanted to leave academia. A kind adviser told me that if I wrote another hundred pages, I would have a PhD for the rest of my life, so I did, right after getting married.

Brad and I moved to San Francisco, and I found work first as a copy editor at dot-coms and a start-up food magazine; eventually, that experience and my passion for cooking got me hired as associate food editor at a major regional magazine, *Sunset.*

When Brad found a tenure-track position at Sacramento State University in 2002, I didn't want to leave my job, and so began the happiest time in our marriage. I lived in San Francisco, and he rented a studio in Sacramento and came back on weekends. I ran every day, swam laps on my lunch break, did yoga, hung out with friends. Seeing each other on weekends was perfect; absence did make the heart grow fonder. But looking back, it seems I wanted a part-time boyfriend, not a husband. I was still playing house.

My carefree life as a magazine editor, though, started to wear thin. Even a dream job is still a job, and as my thirties kicked off, I was increasingly sure I wanted to have a baby. Brad wasn't so sure about having children, but he wanted us to live together, and it was obvious to us both that splitting time between two cities wouldn't work for childrearing. In 2004, I quit my job to move to Sacramento and become a freelance writer. I had Nora a year later. Nearly a decade rushed by, swallowed up with having and raising babies, busy careers, and the trauma of my mother's death. When I turned forty in 2012, emerging from grief, I threw a big party with a taco truck and margaritas to celebrate and usher in what I hoped would be a better decade. It didn't work out that way. Soon, Brad started losing weight rapidly. He looked so good I worried he was having an affair, but then came night sweats and odd lumps under his skin. It took months to get a diagnosis of rare, aggressive lymphoma. Our lives became dominated by anxiety, illness, and the draining sterility of hospital life for months following his bone marrow transplant in 2016, after which he suffered an acute, near-deadly complication called graft-versus-host disease. He lost his vision (which he later regained with surgeries) and the ability to eat, was dangerously immune compromised, and came home in need of twenty-four-hour care. Over time, the strain highlighted our differences instead of bringing us together. In the wake of years of cancer and disability, he retreated so much in self-protection that neither one of us could see how traumatized he was by his illness. I, meanwhile, was worn out by caretaking and what I saw as his unwillingness even to try to be more of a partner to me once he was recovering.

During Brad's illness I had several epiphanies around our balance of household labor. I didn't realize how lopsided it was until his contributions were subtracted from the equation. When he could no longer do his household tasks, little besides taking out the garbage and cleaning up after dinner was added to my plate, and those were rote tasks, not mental labor. We hadn't been operating as a team; I was the manager, and he carried out a few duties to "help." He used to joke about it, in fact, saying I was the general and he the sergeant, I the strategist and he the tactician. After I realized how right he was, those jokes lost any charm for me. I read Eve Rodsky's *Fair Play* and Gemma Hartley's *Fed Up* and Darcy Lockman's *All the Rage: Mothers, Fathers, and the Myth of Equal Partnership* and countless online essays about unequal marriage and its discontents. During the pandemic, I noticed headline after headline about how much household labor had "fallen" on women, a passive framing that always irritated me. Did it fall, or was it pushed by a male partner who refused to notice how much his wife was doing?

When Brad had recovered enough to resume his roles as husband and father, I wasn't interested in going back to our pre-illness pattern; I wanted elusive, mythical equal partnership or nothing, and I wanted it when my husband was utterly unable to be that partner. Those demands probably felt unfair and startling to him; it wasn't his fault he didn't know how to meet my needs and wants. I had made my desires small, even to myself, since the earliest days of our relationship—really, since the earliest days of my life, having absorbed early on that the best way to get love, or at least to not get criticized, was to demand little and be no bother. I didn't have a language for articulating my needs to myself, much less to others. And so, in our two-plus decades of marriage, hardly any of those needs—emotional, physical, practical, sexual—were met. Now, I felt like the guy in the 1976 movie *Network* who goes on an on-air rant encouraging viewers to yell: "I'm as mad as hell, and I'm not going to take this anymore!"

Yelling and throwing things did bring some catharsis, but the nasty satisfaction of letting loose faded fast. As my anger on the road to Jonesville curdled to shame, I got in the passenger side, key fob fragments in hand. Nora, normally a peacemaker, spoke up.

"You're both wrong," she told us. "You're both wrong, and you're both assholes when you fight."

I was shocked not by her language, but by her insight. I was putting my children through the misery I endured witnessing my parents' vicious fights. I'd spent months, years, of therapy sessions wrestling with whether to leave the marriage, but that moment gave me brutal clarity. I turned to the window and stared, blank, conifers and canyon rim flashing by.

Brad took the turnoff to the cabin and passed a landmark that meant we were almost there: the half-circle Fire Danger sign at the Cal Fire station, with colored zones indicating wildfire risk. Its needle pointed to orange: Very High.

~~~

After lunch, I grabbed an axe and headed down to Jones Creek, a tiny spring-fed tributary that runs for a few short miles before joining other streams to feed Butte Creek, which in turn plunges through a deep canyon before meandering across the flat valley to the Sacramento River. I was aiming for my fifth dunk of the project, and Jones Creek is so small and shallow I usually had to build up a little rock dam and then lie down on the bumpy creek bed to submerge. At home, I got itchy and my eyes felt leaden any day I didn't take a shower and wash my hair, but at the cabin, as long as I could get in the creek and emerge shivering and goosebumped and exhilarated, I felt clean and alive. I've always been the only person in the family who submerges often. The kids splash and wade a little, but the creek is too cold for most people.

This year, I had a new idea. Snowmelt from the previous winter had washed away the last year's dam, and my old creek spot was muddy and uninviting. I was too impatient, too mad, and too pressed for time to spend a meditative hour chunking rocks to build up a dipping spot. Upstream, though, willow branches blocked a little slope to the deep outlet from a culvert. It was the spot where each of my daughters had caught their first fish. I would hack down the willows blocking my path and add tree bark and rocks to make rudimentary steps.

The creek water ranges between fifty and fifty-five degrees, but that day was hot enough to lend a frigid dip appeal. The heat was ominous, the warm scent of dry dirt and evergreens underscoring the possibility of yet another bad fire season. The waving green meadow and the spring-fed creek, though, gave
~~~

me hope. Springs bubble up all around Jonesville, a magic jet of optimism in California's constant drought. The water sources are called contact springs, and they honeycomb hillsides, percolating and running at whatever point the water table meets an elevation change. They're easy to spot by the thickets of lush vegetation, tangles of skunk cabbage and willow bushes and graceful Queen Anne's lace that break up the dull hues of dust and dead branches on the forest floor. The cabin's water source was a jerry-rigged, gravity-fed complex of pipes hooked up to an overflowing cistern erected long ago in the middle of such a spot.

The miracle of water spouting freely out of the ground and then sinking back into the aquifer mere feet below the surface always blew my Californian mind. Every time a sink leaked or a hose was left running or we spotted muddy seepage out of the fast-flowing ditch near the cabin, my dad would say the same thing: "I guess you can't really waste water up here."

I worked off my bad mood swinging the axe. It bounced off the tough willows at first, but then they splintered. I pulled and bent them until the resilient green wood cracked at last. Sweaty and red-faced, I waded in. The water in my new spot was thigh deep, and the bubbling stream pouring from the culvert was so fast it pushed me downstream. I gasped and grabbed one of the remaining willow branches as fir needles and pebbly debris swept into my swimsuit. For a second, I could actually float, feet pointing upstream, until the flow pushed my ass hard into a rock. I pulled myself upright and watched pink blotches emerge on my skin as the feeling came back into my limbs with pinpoint prickles. Then I went back for more; three dunks, somehow, always felt complete. I was immersed in more than water: the shock and exhilaration was so intense that it put me right in the moment, erasing the day's angry funk.

It might have felt like cheating to count a creek I had been in dozens of times for my challenge, but the beauty of making up my own rules was that I could count whatever I wanted. This watershed—Butte Creek and its tributaries—was important to me, the water that defines me. In my babyhood my family lived on its banks, and I may ask my children to scatter my ashes there after I die. In the years between, I've eaten its fish, hiked its banks, drunk directly from its springs, waded and dug channels and tubed in it.

The cabin at Jonesville is high above Chico, which sits at the northeastern edge of a vast valley. The creek that runs through town, Big Chico Creek (the name is an oxymoron, since "Chico" means little), forms the spine of a vast municipal park and marks a commonly accepted boundary between the volcanic Cascade Range to the north and the granite-hewn Sierra Nevada to the south. At the spot where these ranges collide, they tilt so steeply that you can gain five thousand feet of elevation in a forty-five-minute drive. Because of that angle, the streams draining those ranges carved deep parallel canyons, with ridges slanting north-northeast, each rimmed with gold grasses and dark outcrops of porous volcanic rock striated like bathtub rings. I never thought much about hydrology growing up, but those canyons and creeks and rocky ridges felt almost like part of me. California State Highway 32, the route to our cabin, crests the ridge dividing Big Chico Creek's watershed to the north and Butte Creek's to the south. South of the next ridge is the vast multiforked Feather River, and the road running up that ridge is the Skyway. It leads to Paradise, the town that gained fame when it burned in the 2018 Camp Fire.

Butte Creek, which has its headwaters a few miles from our cabin, has one of the last naturally spawning populations of spring-run Chinook salmon in California, and I have the urge to return in common with those salmon, swimming their way back upstream. When I was a baby, my parents lived in Butte Creek Canyon, fifteen or so minutes outside of town. (The house also burned in the Camp Fire.) We moved into town when I was two, so I don't remember that house except through photos, stories, and visits to the family friends who bought it from my parents. But I sometimes wonder if my early childhood on the creek imprinted on me somehow, or if maybe it's a normal human response to be drawn to flowing water, a vestigial survival urge.

I was born long enough ago that the canyon house didn't have air-conditioning; my mom told me that the summer she was pregnant with me, she would sit in the creek in an inner tube to cool off. Stoned hippie boys would drift by on tubes and would see her legs and bikini top and would wolf whistle, and all she had to do to make them shut up and flee was to unfurl herself and stand up. I was a ten-pound baby when I emerged in early October, three weeks past my due date, and she had a small frame; the sight of her belly in a bikini must have been impressive.

My mother, Cathy, was a computer programmer and worked for IBM in San Francisco in the late sixties before she and my dad moved to Chico, his hometown. Although she wasn't always the most reliable narrator, she told me plenty of stories—many of them things I probably didn't need to hear—about my early childhood, before I was old enough to remember. She told me that she and my dad had me because all their new young friends in town were having babies and they had been married five years and that is what you did. She also said they got married because they dated all through college, and that was what they were supposed to do after she graduated in 1967. Whether all that is true or not, I was born in 1972. My mother never liked infants much and said it was a relief when I learned to talk, which I did early. I sometimes wonder what she did out there in the canyon, all day, every day. She was not diagnosed as bipolar until the late 1970s, but I'm sure she suffered from depression earlier, and from what she told me of both my and my younger brother's infancy, she likely had postpartum depression as well. I used to have nosebleeds, and she would be terrified she couldn't make them stop when we were so far from the hospital. She had enjoyed putting up wallpaper in the house. She matched the patterns with obsessive perfection. As pioneer narratives go, it's not quite homesteading on the Dakota prairies and pulverizing wheat in a coffee grinder to survive like Laura Ingalls Wilder, but I'm sure the isolation of the canyon wore on her all the same.

When I was younger, I never wondered what was going through my mother's head or asked myself if she was happy. What mattered to me was that she cooked dinners, got me where I needed to be, made our life run. From the opposition between my parents—whom I saw as the responsible, rigid one versus the fun one, though the truth was far more complex—I absorbed unconscious lessons about gender roles. My mom could and did play the pro-women's-lib album *Free to Be You and Me* all she wanted, but its catchy tunes about equal division of housework couldn't overcome what I absorbed every day at home: the woman did nearly all the work and was the one who was judged if anything in the family fell short. Once I became the mom who was judged—or who judged myself—I ruminated, with more compassion than I'd ever shown my mom when she was alive, on how hard it all must have been for her. In fairness to my young and selfish self, most kids don't want to know.

I was fifteen when my parents divorced. In my small town in the 1980s, it still felt a bit disreputable—according to the uninformed, snobby way I perceived class—to have divorced parents, and for most of my childhood my parents were married. My parents' friends were married too (most of them still are), and they all did parent things together: parties where the parents drank and we kids ran a little wild and stayed out of the way, camping trips where we ran fully wild, overnights or day trips for book club to friends' cabins in Jonesville or the closer-by, bigger cabin "town" of Butte Meadows.

On any trip to the mountains, it was imperative to take creek shoes: not the Tevas or water sandals that I buy for my kids now or even flip-flops, which we called thongs then, before that meant underwear. Creek shoes were old tennis shoes, pronounced *tennashoos*, like Keds that had grayed and frayed with busted laces. You could slit them at the toes if you had outgrown them. Somewhere else, kids might have cared about the brand of their tennis shoes, perhaps somewhere where they were called sneakers. In Chico, we didn't. Last year's tennis shoes were valuable, in fact crucial, for wading in a stream of tumbled rock rushed down out of the mountain in worn-smooth granitic ovals and jagged lumps of lava.

On mountain trips, while our moms talked about books or set out potluck three-bean salads and peach cobblers, we kids rode inner tubes down Butte Creek to the general store. Our sodden Keds left wet footprints on uneven pine floorboards while we bought all the licorice and M&Ms and Twix and Whatchamacallits we could carry or afford and trudged back with wet inner tubes and wetter shoes collecting sharp gravel and fir needles. One year, we waded in our creek shoes to dig out channels and make a small archipelago in Jones Creek near my stepcousin Matt's cabin. The islands were unmade a few years later by a spring flood that changed Jones Creek's short course, in the way all shallow young creeks and rivers shift and try new paths.

Back then, my family were visitors. We didn't have a cabin, though my dad always wanted one. After my mother died, the cabin that's now ours came up for sale in Jonesville. My mom had left us an old retirement account my brother and I cashed in to buy the cabin, with our dad contributing another one-third share. Financially, it might have been wiser to save the money, but neither my brother nor I could think of anything better to do with it than to get a place to spend time together. The cabin was filled with spiders and scurrying field mice and mildewing old furniture, but it had built-in bunk beds where we envisioned future cousin sleepovers, a meadow view, and a creek. We jumped at it. My daughters were five and one, and I saw the chance to shape in them the connection to the land I had loved. I wanted my little spawn to be salmon too, with a homing urge back to the creek.

~~~
~~~

Decades ago, the family we bought our cabin from dug a tiny channel, six inches wide and maybe three inches deep, that could flow downhill to the creek from a ditch above. Along the way it filled a tiny concrete-lined pond at the base of the deck, meant for their kids to bring fresh-caught trout to swim until dinnertime. We never caught enough fish to do that, but we filled the pond anyway. The rivulet is blocked by a dam of rocks, piled in the tiny channel; to run the channel, we moved them to a strategic pile in the ditch. Every spring we had to clear the channel, pull out rocks, shore up the edges. When the girls were little, before Brad got cancer, he used to lead them in burying coins and treasure chests to find the next summer.

One afternoon when the girls were maybe seven and three, the three of them were digging, and a hammock hung over the channel. All I wanted to do that day was to lie in that hammock and listen to the lulling flow of the water. Instead, the kids were bickering and there were dishes I had to do and someone else lay in the hammock. I snapped at people and felt put upon, and I'm sure I was very unpleasant. Finally, Brad, as exasperated as I was, asked me, "Do you even like being at the cabin?"

"Of course," I said, but it was more complicated. Like family, the cabin had become part of me, something I loved to my core but didn't always enjoy. Entwined with my love, and something I could never convey to him, was the burden of planning, packing, and cooking, the sheer work of being there. But I adored seeing my children dig and play in the same water I used to dig and play in. I wanted to put on my creek shoes and play too, but it felt hard to snatch the time from obligation.

Even before Brad got sick, I learned how easy it was to be sidelined—or to sideline myself—into the role of responsible killjoy, much as my own mother had. My husband dug in the dirt with the kids and got credit as a fun dad, while I handled bills, chores, and washing those muddy clothes later. Despite the rocky relationship I had with my mother, I was her daughter, and I chose responsibility over fun for much of my life. By the time of my Jonesville dunk on Father's Day, I'd become more sympathetic to her complex rage over the inequities of motherhood, among them how critical I was of her and how forgiving I was of my dad. I saw it in my own girls, who have often had scant tolerance for my lapses, even as they gave their dad all the leeway in the world. It made sense. I was the steady one, the responsible one who kept everything together while they almost lost their dad; they knew I would be there, and they were right. But being there for others, while important, didn't feel like enough. Over time, I let my marriage feed the controlling, no-fun parts of me, and I became controlling and no fun. I had made myself smaller, lost pleasures, lost myself. Where had I gone?

~~~

There is a spot on Butte Creek called Cherry Hill (all hill, no cherries) that I especially love, where the creek takes a sharp bend and the road drops to a bridge over a deep hole. My twelfth birthday party was a chilly October camping trip there. On the way home from the cabin, I like to stop and duck in the creek under the bridge, one last chance to refresh before the long road home.

I stopped as we headed home, rebelling against the kids' protests and Brad's silence. I stripped off my T-shirt, threw
~~~

it onto a boulder, and planted my feet between shifting rocks against the current. I wanted to wade downstream where the creek widened further into a sunny meadow, but I already felt guilty and rushed, even about a five-minute stop. After two hasty dips, I pulled my shirt over my dripping swimsuit and counted it as my sixth dunk.

As I climbed back up the steep bank to the car, I thought of one of my favorite songs, "Side of the Road," by Lucinda Williams. It echoed in my mind whenever I pulled over for an opportunistic roadside dip. The lyrics tell of a woman who needs to be alone, as her lover or partner waits in a stopped car. She sees a farmhouse and wonders if the married couple she imagines there are happy; she says she needs to feel the touch of her own skin, that she might stray away to places she has loved by herself, but that doesn't mean she won't come back. I used to think it was a song of faithfulness, but now I read the lyrics' double negative differently. Taking time to herself doesn't mean the song's narrator won't come back—but it doesn't mean she has to, either. She is making a statement of her completeness, of her whole self, and she is obligated to nobody else. I, too, needed to feel the touch of the water on my own skin, at a place I knew and loved from before I belonged to and was obligated to so many other people. These springs were my headwaters, and I needed to return to them. The shallow creeks, so tied up with my earliest memories, reminded me of that.

The drive home was long and tiresome. My bikini top made wet splotches on my T-shirt, my braids dripped, and I shivered in the air-conditioned silence. Once home, the kids retreated to their rooms, away from their parents' faded rancor. My braids were still damp and cool with Butte Creek water. Both their faint moisture and the pigtails evoked the places I loved most, childhood, freedom.

In the kitchen, I faced my husband. I was so tired of the fighting, of our patterns, of our inability to communicate. I can't remember exactly what I said, but it was something like this: We need to talk about that fight in the car. I can't do this anymore. Nora was right: we were both wrong, and we're assholes when we fight, and we can't seem to find a way to step out of it. I was begging him to understand my perspective on the bigger problem, the underlying gulf between us, our inability to reach each other. But I didn't say it well, and he probably couldn't hear the years of pain beneath my words.

"Well," he said, "you really were tailgating."

CHAPTER TWO

ACROSS THE GREAT DIVIDE

DUNK 9: *Jenny Lake*
DUNK 10: *Teton River*

"I think we should try a trial separation," I said in response to Brad's attempt to relitigate our car fight.

His pale face turned a shade more ashen. "What would that mean?" he said. "You want me to move out?"

"Yes," I said.

"I can't," he said. "Where would I go?"

"I'll help you find a place. But I can't keep doing this."

His shock shocked me in turn. How, I wondered, could he not have known? I'd brought up the idea of separating in endless couples counseling sessions, told him over and over the marriage wasn't working for me, begged him to hear me. Apparently, he hadn't.

"What if I find an office to rent, so I'm gone during the day for writing?" he asked. Since his disability retirement from his work as a professor, we were both home all day, and he argued that more space from each other could solve our problems and my near-constant irritation.

"I think we need to save that money to pay for living space for you," I replied. The money aside, I didn't think an office would solve anything about our marriage. Our house was plenty big. We saw each other little and interacted less. That was part of the problem. I was lonely in my own home, despite being married to the person I ought to have been closest to, but with whom I no longer felt intimacy. Still, I knew him well enough to see how frightened and resistant he was.

Ending my two-decade marriage was not as simple as saying I wanted him to move out. For one thing, we had family vacation plans the following week, in that strange brief pause in summer 2021 when vaccines made it seem COVID-19 was behind us all. It's hard to look back and remember the feeling of hope that spring. It seemed like a summer of fun lay in wait for us all, before the emergence of the Delta variant brought it crashing to a halt. When we'd all been vaccinated, my brother, my dad, and I had hatched a plan to meet up over the Fourth of July in eastern Idaho, across the state line from Grand Teton National Park. I had made a road trip playlist I called "Shot Girl Summer" and googled potential swimming spots along the twelve-hour drive from Sacramento to Victor, Idaho—though they were few and far between in the desert miles of Nevada.

After the pandemic terror and the month of choking smoke and vast lightning complex fires that dominated summer 2020, in June of 2021 it felt miraculous that we could go without N95 masks: the air was clear, and we were vaccinated. But fires had started in Oregon, though not yet in California, and it seemed all but certain that there might be another terrible fire season like 2017 (Santa Rosa's Tubbs Fire), 2018 (the crushing loss of

Paradise in the Camp Fire), and 2020 (too many to count). Our family vacation, an enforced pause in the conflict in our marriage, also felt like limbo, a calm before a storm. We had reached a tenuous détente for the sake of getting on the road with the girls, but we had resolved nothing. Failing to resolve conflict was par for our marriage's course. To add to the foreboding, Nora knew our marriage was hanging by a thread. She overheard our kitchen conversation about separating, and that night my heart had all but broken when she came in to see me at bedtime and begged that if we were going to divorce, we should do it soon, before she left home for college and Lucy was left alone.

With all that strain as a painful backdrop, we were ready for a performance of family fun. By the time we pulled out of the driveway for Idaho, my husband and I were barely on speaking terms, but we had plenty of practice at pretending to move on from resentments that were still simmering, ready to boil over in the next fight.

We set out on a hot July day, to meet my dad and stepmom at our halfway stopping point of Elko, Nevada. After we crossed the Sierra Nevada and descended into the high desert, I cast some longing looks at the slender green thread of the Truckee River, which the interstate follows for forty miles or so, a reminder of old emigrant trails. Making it to that fresh water, after the dusty grind of hundreds of precarious waterless miles, must have felt like hope and glory and life renewed to the overland emigrants to California, and its lushness sustained the Indigenous people who lived in the region for millennia. I looked for a spot to sneak into the water, but I never saw an opportunity. The barren miles of sagebrush and distant crinkled hills rolled by, dull staring at them broken up by occasional halfhearted games of Twenty Questions.

My kids hated Nevada, and especially hated Elko. "Mom, it's so gross," they said when we pulled into the parking lot. "It smells like old sweat."

"That's the sagebrush," I said. "I kind of like it." To me, it was herbaceous, sharp, dry as the desert air.

Worse came inside the ancient, grimy casino in our cheap chain hotel, its walls yellow gray from decades of cigarette smoke. The girls had never lived in a world with indoor smoking, and they were horrified at the thick pall downstairs and the faint clinging odor even in our nonsmoking room.

"Ewww," said Nora.

"Why does everything smell like smoke?" asked Lucy.

"Welcome to my childhood," I said. "Back then there were smoking sections even on airplanes!" They rolled their eyes. "Seriously, Nevada won't ban indoor smoking in casinos, because they profit from it, and the ground floor of this hotel is a casino, so there you go."

It didn't placate them when I said Elko was the best roadside stop available on the long, arid I-80 corridor. (I've spent nights in Winnemucca and Battle Mountain.) Elko would be a photographer's paradise—its dramatic vistas, crumbling buildings, and flashing neon add up to picturesque seedy Americana in decline—but its marquee attraction the Star Hotel. The Star is a Basque restaurant, a holdover from when boarding houses sprang up around the rural West to serve immigrant sheepherders. Basque eateries remain from Bakersfield and Fresno north to Idaho. (In Reno, one place survived with a casino built around it because the owners refused to sell to Harrah's.) They all serve multicourse, meaty meals in gargantuan portions—soup followed by salad followed by oxtail stew followed by garlic lamb chops or baked lamb or steak or salmon with bread and fries and beans and pasta.

The Star was hopping when we rolled up. None of us had realized that over Fourth of July weekend, Elko hosts an annual Basque festival. The bar was full of men speaking Basque and drinking lethal, brandy-based Picon punch, the cocktail every Basque restaurant serves. My kids were again appalled, this time by pro-Trump signs and the long wait, but I was enjoying the atmosphere and excited to order the baked lamb. Its garlicky, fall-off-the-bone tender chunks of lamb neck and stew meat reminded me of the annual Lamb Barbecue when I was a kid. My grandfather worked as a ranch foreman and was the president of the Butte County Woolgrowers Association, an organization that no longer exists. At the Lamb Barbecue, the men of the Woolgrowers Association served up lamb burgers, lamb neck stew, and grilled chops. Kids played, adults drank, and we all ate as much lamb as we wanted. Live lambs grazed in a pen for attendees to guess the weight and win a pelt or their meat. Not until I wrote a story about Basque restaurants as an adult did I realize that the menu at the Lamb Barbecue must have been influenced by Basque food traditions.

I sucked down one too many Picon punches during the wait, and back at the hotel I was alarmed at a knock at the door of one of our adjoining rooms. A hotel worker stood there.

"Ma'am, you aren't supposed to be in this room," he said.

"What do you mean? I got the keys for both rooms when we checked in."

"I don't have a record of your reservation or check-in. You'll need to vacate this room immediately," he replied.

I looked around. The girls and Brad had pretty much exploded their suitcases all over the room, belongings scattered everywhere.

"But I reserved adjoining rooms, prepaid for both, and checked in hours ago," I repeated, louder. "You gave me the keys."

"There was a mistake," he said. "You'll need to surrender the keys immediately and vacate."

"What the actual fuck," I responded, again louder. "I paid for two rooms and we're in both of them."

"Well, I have no record of your payment or registration for this one," he said. "Give me the key right now and vacate the room. Leave your belongings. We'll pack them up for you."

"The hell I fucking will," I said, yelling now. "It's not my problem you and your staff are incompetent. Go check your records. Or, wait, hold on. I have the reservation right here." I opened my phone, but I was incensed and far from sober and struggled to find the email confirmation.

"Ma'am, there's no need to be abusive." He had raised his voice too. "You're not supposed to be in this room, and if you don't leave, we'll call the police."

"Are you fucking kidding me? I'll call the fucking police! Is this some kind of scam? Are you going to steal our stuff? My laptop is in there! I'm not leaving!"

The hotel had a central atrium, and several doors had popped open at the sound of yelling, to see who was embarrassing themselves. I knew it was me, but rage and adrenaline had flooded my body.

At this point, Brad stepped forward. "Kate," he said in his most placid, reasonable Canadian voice. "Why don't you go back in the other room and I'll talk to him."

"You won't be any help," I snarled at him.

"You're drunk," he hissed at me, then turned to the hotel staffer. "Sir, I'm so sorry. How about I go downstairs with you and we look at your records and sort this out."

"Don't apologize to him! It's their fault!" I was so angry I couldn't even be grateful he was solving the problem, but after a moment I thought again. "I'll find the confirmation and forward it to you!" I yelled after them.

"Lady, would you shut the hell up?" shouted someone from a floor below.

In part because my mother had been so volatile, and in part because of my own constant rage, to me then it seemed normal to sometimes get so angry you screamed at your spouse, or a stranger in a hotel. I didn't realize the damage I was doing to my relationships, especially with my kids, or to my own emotional health by not learning to control the toxic anger that bubbled up so fast. But I was starting to realize that this was no way to live, no way to raise my daughters. My rage came from deep hurt, which in turn stemmed from my inability to ask for my needs to be met or see my part in the patterns that made my marriage so unfulfilling. I was, every day, setting myself up to be more miserable.

We set out the next morning tired, my hangover worsened by watery, floppy eggs and hash browns tinged orange by rancid grease from the hotel's vintage diner. Nobody was excited about another six hours on the road. We hightailed it northeast and hit the mighty Snake River, following its various reservoirs and gorges and forks and branches for miles, always high above the mighty rushing waterway, with no access for a break from the road. When we got close to our destination, though, I saw a boat ramp down. I wanted to stop but knew that would press my road-weary family too hard. A dip would have to wait.

After bleak Nevada, eastern Idaho's Teton Valley was a lovely fertile meadowed plain, dotted with conifers and aspens, watered by the meandering Teton River. The valley lies on the back side of the Grand Tetons, accessible via a twisty pass into Wyoming a few miles from where we were staying, a ranch-like resort with condos, vacation homes for rent, a golf course, pickleball, and a pool. Our rental was a massive, ersatz log "cabin," like an architectural version of the show *Yellowstone*, in the style that telegraphs money in the mountain West, with imposing thick-hewn wood and leather furniture. The girls shared an upstairs bedroom, and Brad and I slept in the two bedrooms on a lower floor that opened to a view. We had slept apart for years. It started for practical reasons during his cancer treatment and in the wake of his bone marrow transplant, when he needed IV medications overnight, a separate bathroom, and in-home care workers looking after him round the clock. When he recovered, we briefly attempted to sleep in the same bed, but before too long he had moved back downstairs to the guest room, which had its own bathroom—upstairs, there was a single bathroom shared with our daughters—and fewer stairs to navigate.

Separate bedrooms further undermined what little physical intimacy we had left in the wake of his illness and my caregiving. For a long time Brad was medically prohibited from sex; as for me, there's nothing quite like hearing that your partner's semen is toxic from chemo to kill desire. The small intimacies of nonsexual touch might have sustained us, but those were never our strong suit. He never liked to hold hands and often walked a few steps ahead of me. Before we were married, he once told me he didn't like the way I kissed. The shame and pain of that comment echoed in my head for years, though I didn't talk about it with him, except to bring it up in anger during fights. Instead, over time even pecks on the cheek trailed off. Looking back, we were almost always sleeping alone even in the same bed. We rarely cuddled, though before he got sick, I sometimes lay my head on the left side of his chest. The port he had to have for years after his transplant occupied the precise hollow my head once fit into.

Better sexual communication on both sides might have improved things, but I felt a strange, mute chill around discussing our physical life. I had long felt our sex life was fine, but I never stopped to think whether I might have the capacity and wish for a sex life that rated higher than that. The intensity of his illness and my caregiving stripped away so much—the buzz and routine of daily interactions, the context of social life, the fraught partnership of parenting—that it revealed the weakness of our underlying bond. In the wake of the hard caregiving years, I wanted a partnership that was more fulfilling than what we had before just as I wanted a more equitable division of household labor. Unfortunately, as with all my new desires, I wanted that when we were far below our previous baseline and Brad had the least capacity to meet the needs I was beginning to understand and express. That dynamic replicated itself across many aspects of our relationship, but it was most painful to me in our physical drought. I wanted hand holding, kisses, hugs, the occasional ass grab in the kitchen. A return to desire, and a better understanding of my own sexual capacities and need for touch, was dawning on me, in tandem with the ways the waters of my fifty dunks were carrying me back to my body and its needs. I became so hungry for both touch and care that I started to fantasize about being held. I had a recurring dream in which I was cradled in an anonymous, genderless lap, its abstract body's arms wrapped around me. I later learned a term for that yearning: skin hunger.

The obvious metaphor here to the physical pleasures of swimming aside, there was also an unconscious midlife appeal to wetness, a compensation for the way perimenopause was drying up my once-oily skin and hair. (Perimenopause refers to the unpredictable stage leading up to menopause, which applies after periods have ceased for a full year.) Perimenopause often brings vaginal dryness as well, but it was hard for me to tell because I was experiencing days, weeks, and then months of spotting and bleeding. There were few treatment options—no surprise, as women's health and perimenopausal symptoms are understudied and undertreated. As Jancee Dunn writes in *Hot and Bothered*, "Perimenopausal women can spend several years trying to get the right diagnosis and treatment. Medicine, of course, has a long history of telling women that their symptoms are all in their heads." Moreover, doctors get little tutelage in this life stage; as Heather Corinna notes in *What Fresh Hell Is This?*, "Only about 20 percent of OB/GYN residency programs include menopause training, and it's often elective." The first-line treatment for my bleeding would have been an IUD with hormones, but I'd had one for years and was bleeding anyway. The next possibility was progestin pills, which didn't stop the bleeding but did add to my emotional volatility. The remaining treatment option was surgery, which scared me. My last surgery had been getting my wisdom teeth out at eighteen, and making myself vulnerable, asking for pain, was terrifying. I wasn't sure how to fit recovery from major surgery in between the demands of caretaking. I started thinking that I had better get it done soon, while I still had a husband around to run errands and drive the girls to school and take care of me.

A few days before our road trip, I went for a long-awaited presurgical consult. An ultrasound confirmed I had fibroids that were causing the bleeding, the biggest a couple of centimeters in diameter. My mother had a hysterectomy for the same reason at the same age, but I didn't ask her many questions about it, though she tried to tell me. Her middle-aged bodily problems and bleeding seemed embarrassing and irrelevant to me. Now I wished I'd listened. There's been a robust cultural dialogue about menopause in recent years, with countless writers asking why nobody ever told them about it. While I agree that there's too much shame and stigma around this life stage, sometimes I wonder if women like my mom were trying to tell us all along, but with the arrogance of youth, my generation didn't want to hear it, just as the generation after us is too busy dealing with being young to worry about getting old.

The placement of my fibroids meant a hysterectomy was the best option for their removal. Make no mistake, I was all done with my uterus. Like my husband, it had given me two great children. Like my husband, it now seemed to cause me near-constant low-level pain and to bleed me dry, drop by drop. But surgery, like divorce, sounded like a prolonged nightmare, and I had been through enough of those in the past dozen years or so. The surgeon explained my options: they could leave my ovaries to produce hormones, so I wouldn't be thrown into instant menopause; the surgery could be laparoscopic, and thus minimally invasive; I would go home the same day; recovery was six to eight weeks. I was agog that removing a major organ was an outpatient procedure, but aside from that, it didn't sound so bad. I said I wanted to do it.

As part of the preop protocol, they had to ensure I didn't have uterine cancer. (Any cancer would get spread around when they pulverized the uterus to remove it during laparoscopic surgery.) The doctor offered me an endometrial biopsy on the spot. I consented to that too. A public service announcement: if you have a uterus and anyone offers you a surprise endometrial biopsy without painkillers, for the love of god, say no. Insist on as much pain relief as they'll give you. The medical staff who said I'd feel "a pinch" were either delusional or dismissive of women's pain—as recent studies, not to mention countless anecdotes from actual women, show many medical professionals are. I've given birth without an epidural to two babies, one of them ten pounds, and I almost passed out from the pain of that biopsy. I spent the next two days mainly in bed, and I bled or spotted daily for the next four months.

On the Idaho trip, I bled every day, and it was unpredictable: sometimes a light spot or two, sometimes the gush of thick, almost black clots like something from a horror film—another reason I appreciated having my own bedroom and bathroom. It feels like half my memories from that trip are of checking whether I had bled through tampons, planning how to participate in activities, downing more Advil for gut-twisting cramps. As the bleeding ramped up during the trip, I sent a MyChart message to the gynecology practice, asking about relief for the increased bleeding. A nurse replied that bleeding was only a concern if I started passing clots larger than a lemon, in which case I should go to ER.

I found that answer both callous and ridiculous. She offered no half measures, no compassion; my options were to bleed like an animal, untreated (it's just an inconvenience, after all), or seek emergency care. If I were to go to the ER and tell them I was in my late forties and I had a heavy period, they would have laughed me out of the building. The idea that there's no middle ground between "you're fine" and "go to ER"—no acceptable standard for treating women's life-limiting discomfort and pain unless it might kill them—is one more way the medical system does wrong by women. And why is the world of gynecology so obsessed with fruit? When I was pregnant, the fetus was the size of a blueberry, a raspberry, a strawberry, all the way up to a watermelon. When I was recovering from childbirth, I was supposed to call the doctor if clots were larger than a plum. Now lemons? What kind of lemon? A big supermarket Eureka lemon or a small Meyer from my backyard tree? I begged for more aid and again was told to increase the progestin dose.

My hysterectomy was scheduled for November. With both my reproductive system and my marriage, I was afraid of the pain of ending things. But in both cases, the costs and fears of the status quo were higher. The misery of denying my full self was starting to outweigh my fears, and I was starting—just starting—to feel ready to be whole again. As the poet Maggie Smith writes in her divorce memoir *You Could Make This Place Beautiful*, "I'd been trying to save the marriage, but I needed to save myself."

~

If Brad and I operated separately at home, the distance between us was even more acute on vacation. I didn't blame him for not being up for a float trip down the Teton River or a big hike in Grand Teton National Park, but I did want to do those things. Long before Brad got sick, our different vacation and travel priorities—especially when it came to anything outdoors—had led to conflict. He used to call me indomitable and tease me that hikes became death marches, with the pronouncement "There's a fine line between an adventure and an ordeal." The line between the two is different for everyone, and Brad's and my line had diverged: for him, it was all ordeal. I, however, was starved for even the most modest adventure.

Our divide was most obvious on a day trip with my brother's family to Grand Teton National Park. I watched with mild envy as my brother and his wife, who make a formidable team, worked together to pack up the car, while calling each other "babe." Brad and I had never used many terms of endearment, though he had started calling me "friend," which left me cold. I told him I'd prefer something more affectionate or romantic, but he persisted.

I'd researched park destinations with a swim, and settled on Jenny Lake, which had a ferry to a short trail up to a waterfall, something even the smallest cousin could handle. The parking lot was overflowing, with parked vehicles stretching at least a half mile down the road. I cursed myself for not bringing Brad's handicapped parking placard. A long walk from a faraway parking spot would have been challenging for him, so I circled the packed lot, hopeless. The day out—and my swim—seemed doomed before they began. But then I got one of the top ten parking finds of my life: I spotted a lady by her car smoking a cigarette and asked if she was staying or going. She said leaving, but it might take her a couple minutes to finish her smoke. I wouldn't have minded if she had finished the pack, as long as I could get her prime spot.

We lined up for a boat ride across the lake, which was as spectacular as promised, a mirror for surrounding jagged rocky peaks, with a pale turquoise clarity to the water. Our party included eight: me, Brad, my brother Peter (Pete for short) and sister-in-law Evalani, their kids Alana and Kai (then ten and four), and ours. After the breezy ride across the lake, we docked for the short half-mile walk to the waterfall, and Brad said he would sit and wait for us at the docking point, grumbling that there wasn't enough shade for his sun-sensitive skin. I didn't understand why he declined to take the boat back to the lodge and wait indoors in comfort, since he was waiting anyway.

Once we got to the waterfall and hiked back down, we could either return by boat to the main dock or do a lakeshore hike back: 5 miles the long way, 2.5 miles the short way. I'd hoped the girls would come with me on the hike, but the husbands and all the kids chose the boat ride. Evalani and I chose the shorter hike. The hike, level with the lakeshore, was relatively easy and we set a fast pace—at least, fast for me—out of guilt over our families' wait. My enjoyment of the bluebird skies poked by slate-hued peaks, the glimpses of cerulean water, the Christmastime scent of the forest were all tempered by the knowledge that I'd face the silent treatment or a sulky comment later.

We paused anyway at a small beach close to the end of the hike. I waded out in my swim shorts, expecting a shock, but the water was refreshing, a cool mirror, not the bone-jolting cold I expected at that altitude. I dived under to feel the slippery rush over my face and popped up again, reflections rippling around me, and flipped onto my back to float and stare at the wispy wraiths of clouds disintegrating and reforming high above. I was distracted, though; every time I surfaced, I remembered the trail and our cranky waiting families. I felt both guilt and defiance: guilt for keeping everyone waiting, defiance when I thought about how seldom I ever claimed my own time and space. My "free" time always came with a cost.

That cost was one of the things that made my fifty dunks a challenge, not just a pleasure. Going to a swimming hole usually meant a day trip, sometimes an overnight away. Claiming large chunks of time where we are unreachable is rare for women. Recent research shows that men's leisure, including stereotypical activities such as golf and fishing, takes place away from home and thus is uninterrupted and all recreational. Women's leisure pursuits, on the other hand, tend to have some kind of value to the family (gardening, knitting, cooking), to be home based, and to be interruptible by the needs and whims of children and partners. My family's experience provides one small data point: Any time we were visiting Brad's family, "the men" (as my mother-in-law said) went for a round of golf while we waited at home with the kids. In Brad's and my early years of parenthood in Sacramento, he remained a member of a street hockey league in San Francisco, two hours' drive away. He spent almost every Saturday there, while I remained home with Nora. After Lucy was born and I spent a couple of solo Saturdays with everyone crying, I begged him to stop.

Research shows quantitative gender differences in leisure (in short: men take more time to themselves), but as Anne Helen Petersen points out in her Substack *Culture Study*, "There are qualitative differences in leisure, too—women's leisure is often 'constrained,' aka, there is a driving pressure and/or guilt to get back to other responsibilities, which degrade the restorative and essential quality of the leisure. (Staring into space can provide the same restorative quality as, say, golfing; what matters, to bluntly paraphrase leisure scholars, is that you're not constantly feeling like shit about the fact that you're doing it, and/or a failure as a person or parent.)" I often felt like shit about time I took for myself because time was limited and the needs of my family, especially in the years when Brad was sick, were unlimited. When I started taking more regular trips to swimming holes—many of them out of cell phone range—I apologized at first. Then I stopped. I was learning not to feel shitty about claiming my time.

~

There was one dunk that got away on that trip. I dreamed about the Parting of the Waters at Two Ocean Creek, a tiny rivulet deep in a wilderness area in northwest Wyoming that rises on the Continental Divide and splits, so that half its waters run to the Atlantic Ocean and half to the Pacific. The symbolism of it pulled me hard, the more so because of an old Kate Wolf song, "Across the Great Divide," which I used to sing to the girls at bedtime. (I know it from a beautiful version by Nanci Griffith on her '90s cover album *Other Voices, Other Rooms*.) It's a song of life change, and I was here on the precipice of a big one. It wasn't as if I thought Two Ocean Creek would knit my divided parts into a whole, but I wanted to chase that wish along with bragging rights of seeing something few even know about. But I didn't propose it. It would have required a fifteen-mile hike into the wilderness, so I would have needed to backpack overnight, bring gear, possibly recruit a companion, and burn most of our family vacation on a quixotic whim. I stuffed that idea far, far down, but it chafed a little as I saw my husband's annoyance about the extra hour or so I took to hike and swim while he and the kids had lunch and browsed the gift shop. Nobody likes to wait around, but the time I was carving out seemed so small compared to the amount I yearned for, much less the amount I gave to them.

Back at the gift shop, I browsed with the girls for Christmas ornaments, our standard family souvenir. Years before, I had suggested we get an ornament on every trip, in part as a defense against being begged for stuffed animals or overpriced T-shirts, and in part with the idea that it would be meaningful to look back on family vacations every year. Women make the lion's share of holiday magic, and that was true in my home; I took on that gendered labor almost unconsciously. I rejected newfangled non-traditions that seemed like a social media competition—Elf on the Shelf, I'm looking at you—but every December, I felt like a cross between Santa and an overbooked cruise director. Vacation-bought tree decorations were one small piece of it all but a telling one. The hanging of ornaments, the forced reminiscing, packing and unpacking the fragile little baubles: it all started to feel like I was a dancing monkey, moving faster and faster to try to make it seem like we were a Happy! Family!

With Warm! Traditions! I hated how performative I felt, but I also couldn't drop the act.

The girls picked out a stained-glass ornament with a striped rainbow design and park logo, and I paid for it, picturing it catching the twinkling light of a Christmas tree. We piled back in the car and traced a slow loop around the park, just to say we had seen more than a single lake. We passed a sign pointing to Two Ocean Lake, and I got excited, thinking my Continental Divide plunge could be closer than I realized. Googling over spotty cell service, however, I learned it was a reservoir, named for the forking creek, but its waters flowed only to the Pacific. A misnomer, and a false coupling, with one half of the pairing only a shadow.

Before leaving Grand Teton, we stopped at Oxbow Bend, a pullout known for wildlife viewing and named for a curved former section of the Snake River. An oxbow bend, with its looping crescent shape, occurs when a river winds through a flat plain. They're common in long alluvial rivers like the Mississippi but rarer in my part of the West, where streams rocket down canyons. The Snake and its tributaries include oxbows where they traverse wide valleys. During floods, these near-circular river bends can close their loops, cutting off old oxbows, which become isolated lakes as the former channel silts up. The river remnants may become marshy wetlands or evaporate over time. Although they serve an important ecological purpose as habitats and by trapping sediment, runoff, and contamination, oxbows evince a river that has found a better way, sometimes with human intervention to straighten its course and sometimes by getting so turned around it loops to meet its past self. As we watched elk graze and a small bear gambol, it didn't occur to me that I, too, was looping around, soon to meet an old channel I'd outgrown. My best hope was to settle into a straighter, better course for my life, silt up the channels, and filter away my anger and resentment.

The next day included a closer-up examination of oxbows: a float on the Teton River, a wiggling tributary of the Snake. Brad stayed behind, as did Nora, who was participating in an ill-timed virtual debate camp. The river flowed peaceful and near featureless through grasslands so thick they obscured the river even from a stone's throw away. I paddled my bright blue inflatable boat almost in circles as the river doubled back on itself. In the pancake-flat valley, it might have been hard to sense the bends' sharpness if not for the landmark of the Tetons' towering rock crags coming into view time and again. We passed a moose mother and calf, bigger and uglier than I would have imagined, their placid gaze faintly hostile. In spots, the river's loops closed in a circle, and different parts of the family took different channels. When we reconvened for lunch, Lucy and I waded out in the swift silent flow, thigh deep for most of our float, and lay down to refresh ourselves from paddling in the sun. The light slanted and rippled through the water, and I surveyed our family group: Pete and Evalani in one boat with their small son, Lucy giggling in another with her cousin, my dad and his wife together, me in a boat of my own. I felt Nora's absence but not my husband's. I had been paddling my own boat for years.

The rest of vacation passed quietly: Lucy begged to stay up late and go see *Black Widow*, the new Marvel movie, at a quaint drive-in called The Spud. I took the girls into town for thrift shopping and huckleberry milkshakes. Brad busted out some craft kits he'd brought to do with the kids. I did an intricate map-of-the-world jigsaw puzzle. On the last night, at the golden hour, my sister-in-law arranged us in a group for the all-family photo she takes at every major gathering. Behind us, the sky flamed pink and hazy, the sun an orange disk after a clear blue week. I shuddered. The toxic odor of Oregon's fires had rolled in, all too familiar, and the ashy smell evoked the fear of what fire season might be like at home. The smoke-filtered light lent a deceptive glow to our family photo. I wondered if it would be the last such memento with Brad in it and did my best to smile.

CHAPTER THREE

TAMED AND SCENIC RIVERS

DUNK 11: *Natural Bridges*
DUNK 12: *Lower American River*
DUNK 13: *North Fork American River*

Unwilling to spend another night in central Nevada, we did the twelve-hour drive home in a single day, tracing the mighty Snake before a mad dash across the barren Great Basin to the green Truckee River, over Donner Pass, and then down the north fork of the American River. It was a relief to leave the haze behind and reach skies that were clear and blue—at least for a little while. We arrived bedraggled, with a car full of snack wrappers and half-drunk cups of gas station coffee. The next day, I unpacked and I tried to figure out how to get back to normal and what that might even mean. I had planned a swimming date with an old friend, but she canceled, to my relief. I returned to a busy week promoting *Already Toast*—being on podcasts and giving talks—and I had another meeting looming. It looked innocent enough on the shared Google family calendar: coffee with Jill B., 9 a.m. on Wednesday.

That calendar entry was a ruse. I do have a friend named Jill with the last initial B, and that Jill, recently divorced, was becoming a mentor on my slow path to leaving my marriage. That Wednesday meeting wasn't coffee with my pal; it was an appointment with a divorce lawyer named Jill, whose last name also happened to start with B. I wanted to understand my rights and how a division of property might work. A legal assistant did offer me coffee at the meeting, but the calendar entry was obfuscatory at best, even though for all the interest Brad took in my doings I probably could have put DIVORCE LAWYER in bright red all caps.

I also didn't tell him about the book waiting for me on the front porch when we got home, a self-help title called *Too Good to Leave, Too Bad to Stay* recommended by another divorced friend. I couldn't find it in the library, and Brad and I shared an Amazon account, so I had a friend order it for me. Here's a hint: If you're surreptitiously ordering books about whether you want a divorce, you want a divorce. I wasn't the only one keeping secrets. That same week, Brad toured offices for rent, despite the conversation in which I had said I didn't think renting an office would help anything and we shouldn't spend the money. He signed a two-year lease. When he told me about it after the fact, he said it was $400 a month. (Later, in divorce negotiations, I learned it was actually $500.)

We had dropped the topic of separating—though not the tension—on vacation, but there was no getting around living with each other. As soon as we got home, we returned to our stalemate.

"What if we lived as roommates until Lucy finishes high school?" he asked.

"Lucy just finished *sixth grade*," I emphasized. "That's six years." I was forty-eight, soon to turn forty-nine; I didn't want to wait until I was fifty-five to end our dreary, sexless détente.

"I think it could work," he said.

"No offense," I said, opening with a glaring admission that what I was about to say was offensive, "but we were never good roommates." I thought back to tripping over his piles of papers in that first tiny cottage we rented together, to the fights we had over how to keep our spaces, to my annoyance at the hockey jerseys he hung on the walls with thumbtacks, and knew I wanted my own space.

Mindful of Nora's plaintive request that we split before she left for college, I also wondered how it would feel to the kids if we divorced the minute we became empty nesters. Of course they didn't want us to split up while they were still at home, and I didn't want to replicate my own family's dysfunction, but would separating then make their childhoods and our family look like a sham? They had been through so much with Brad's illness. But I knew someday my daughters would be adult women. I didn't want them to think that loneliness and separate lives were the best they could expect from marriage. Even less did I want them to aspire to a lifetime of sacrificing and shrinking the most joyous parts of themselves.

Aside from my worry about the girls, I struggled with guilt over what people would think of me separating from a man who had been so ill. After all, I had just published a book about my life as a caregiver. I'd concluded it on an ambivalent note about our marriage, but leaving him seemed like a terrible ending. Still, we were, as Brad implied, little better than roommates, and we functioned best as coparents. Much later, I would read advice about when to end a marriage on an issue of Anne Helen Petersen's Substack in which she asked divorced people how they knew when to throw in the towel, and one replied, "The best time to move on is before the children have no positive role models left to help them understand relationships. Leave before there is nothing left to leave." Somewhere deep inside me, I had known there was already nothing left by the time I asked to separate.

The Wednesday of my fake coffee date was also the first I heard of the wildfire that would become my obsession that summer. The Dixie Fire started on July 13 in the Feather River Canyon, a couple of miles from the starting point of 2018's Camp Fire. Named for nearby Dixie Road, the fire started off slow but soon crossed the bulwark of the Sierra Nevada from west to east, penetrating north into the Cascades past Mount Lassen, and swallowing up whole towns. Although these remote parts of northern California have made national news as ground zero for climate change more than once, they are still so little known that it's hard to convey how shocking these distances are, how diverse the terrain the Dixie Fire torched: from steep mountain canyons to the Great Basin's high desert, alpine meadows to cattle rangeland.

At first, the fire was a mere spark from a Pacific Gas & Electric power line. It took ten hours for a PG&E troubleman—an ominously named role—to get to the remote site to investigate. He tried to extinguish the small fire he found nearby, and firefighting aircraft were dispatched, but a drone blocked their efforts and the inhospitable terrain prevented on-the-ground firefighting. By morning, the fire was five hundred acres. Pete (a former wildland firefighter) and his family were still making their way home from Idaho. I sent him a text that morning: "Ugh, there is a fire in Feather River Canyon." He replied, "Yes, I saw." No hint that this fire would affect us, much less dominate our summer. But that's the thing about wildfires. Like fights in a marriage or the urge to change one's life, they're touched off by a tiny spark, and you can't tell whether they'll smolder out, or catch and blow up.

My brother and I have long texted near daily, reporting our Wordle scores or carping about the Spelling Bee, and we talk often. We didn't text again about the fire for a few days, as winds pushed it northeast. By July 17, the winds had changed. The fire made a run west, threatening Jonesville and Butte Meadows. Pete was up at the cabin, removing propane tanks and running sprinklers, when a mandatory evacuation order came. He grabbed a few things we wouldn't want to lose, including our logbooks filled with notes and sketches of a decade of family visits, and got out. It pained me that summer to think of the things he had to leave behind, including our grandfather's ancient Jeep, a quilt I hand sewed, and paintings our kids had done on lazy cabin afternoons. I knew they were just things, and it was just a cabin, one we were lucky to have. Our homes weren't threatened. I tried to keep that privilege in mind as Pete and I both streamed morning firefighting briefings on YouTube and checked wind forecasts, but my heart was in my throat for our beloved, remote corner of California. Our texts for the rest of the summer were mainly about the fire: would the winds change, would Jonesville survive, would it burn through the town of Chester (no), would it reach the shores of Lake Almanor (yes), would it burn through Lassen Volcanic National Park (some of it). All these places held memories for me and my family.

My old favorite campground lay in the burn zone. Our trips there when I was a child all started the same way: a long drive in our International Scout, a clunky ancestor of today's SUVs, with my thighs stuck to the black seats and the hot smells of exhaust and our dog Sunny's panting breath mingling. We rattled down a long rocky slope, tan dust billowing behind. Ahead lay the Humbug Valley in Plumas County, bisected by a fast-running trout stream called Yellow Creek. In the middle of the valley stood an open-air hut over an alkaline soda spring. We'd stop there and drink for the novelty, the smell of rust hitting my nose before the water in my cupped hands fizzed and tickled it. Then we went on to the old PG&E-run campground to grab a prime spot by the rushing creek. We cut and whittled green willow branches for marshmallow-roasting sticks, waded waist deep, ran down to the soda spring, and investigated the acorn-grinding rocks left by the Maidu, the region's Indigenous people.

In 2019, PG&E transferred more than two thousand acres of the valley—known to the Maidu as Tásmam Koyóm—back to the Mountain Maidu people, its original stewards. The Maidu Summit Consortium, which now manages the land, has put up a stone marker describing the valley's Indigenous cultural heritage at the soda springs and is working toward a Maidu cultural park in the area. California has always had wildfire, and its Indigenous people managed it effectively for millennia; it now feels both like a bitter irony that a PG&E-caused fire burned the homeland PG&E had returned to its people, and also reassuring and right that its recovery is in the hands of its longtime caretakers. In recent years, at long last, Cal Fire and other fire agencies have begun consulting with Indigenous groups about how to tend the land and work with so-called good fire in periodic low-intensity burns, rather than suppressing it for generations only to spark megafires like the Dixie, which swept through Tásmam Koyóm.

Thanks to the fire, Yellow Creek never became one of my fifty dunks. I drove through the valley the next year; the grass had turned green again, but blackened, spindly tree trunks marred its beauty, and the campground was closed then. (The Mountain Maidu people now manage it, and it has since reopened.) The rolling acres of ashy toothpicks still extend all the way to Jonesville. The enormous footprint of the Dixie Fire also happened to cut me off from many swimming holes I wanted to visit—the tiniest of losses but one that added to my trapped-rat feeling as COVID cases spiked, smoke settled over Sacramento, and fires scuttled my visions of remote waterfalls, clear green pools in distant rivers, or sapphire-bright alpine lakes.

In California, water is everything: controversy, danger, politics, money, joy, beauty, life. Our drought seasons are disastrously dry; our big water years are awe-inspiring and frightening when snowmelt threatens to overtop the state's complex reservoirs and levees. A big water year delays river-swimming season; the rivers may look calm, but fast, frigid snowmelt can kill you in a heartbeat. A bad water year means scummy puddles, algae-covered rocks, and wildfire-tainted air by July. The timing of my project's start gave me a little over a year and a half to get to fifty swims—about one excursion a week during the warmer months. California weather gave me off-season opportunities, but fires and drought cut off others. Throughout July and August, I wasn't keeping on pace for the weekly swims I had planned. Even though the Dixie Fire prohibited expeditions only to the northeast, it cast a pall.

I itched to get out of Sacramento, but I had trouble motivating myself. I managed only one July swim after returning from Idaho, a group outing with friends and Lucy to an underground cavern called Natural Bridges, in Calaveras County to the southeast. We crossed one bone-dry creek bed after another on the way, a sign of the drought. After crunching down a rocky canyon trail, we found an unpromising trickle of slimy puddles. A cave entrance, however, beckoned. Inside lay a glorious underground swimming hole, with a series of arched spaces like chapels in an eerie cathedral stretching back to a faint light filtering in; what looked like a cave was a tunnel, filled with a wide slow-moving creek. Stalactites dripped with water seeping through the limestone. We splashed in, floating on the gentle current. It felt like a lazy river at an enchanted, surreal amusement park. After the drought-ridden mess of a creek outside the cave, the deep underground pools were a reminder that even in drought, relief may hide anywhere.

~

In the summer of my discontent, I almost overlooked the waters closest to me. Sacramento lies at the bottom of the trough of the massive Central Valley, very close to where California's major rivers come together in the knot of the Delta and flow to the San Francisco Bay and then the Pacific. I live a mile as the crow flies from the Lower American River, the only federally designated Wild and Scenic River that runs through urban spaces for its whole length. I don't see it every day, though; it's walled off by levees.

It's easy to forget the degree to which rivers and drainages literally shape our lives, outlining roads and situating cities. Sacramento is only where it is, and only the capital of the state, because of the American River and its confluence with the Sacramento, which let gold seekers come up from the San Francisco Bay in the days when there were no reliable roads. The American is the river where gold was discovered, and its multiple forks fan out across the rich Mother Lode, carving deep canyons and tumbling in world-class rapids over the Sierra's trademark granite.

In the suburbs east of Sacramento, all those forks converge in vast Folsom Lake, one of California's largest reservoirs. Folsom Dam's released water flows into Lake Natoma—a long, snaking reservoir in heavy use by paddleboarders, kayakers, and rowers—and then gently descends and winds through the suburbs as the Lower American. It's flanked by a greenbelt, a beloved bike trail, and steep levees that protect the city from the regular floods it endured in its first century, before the huge wetland of the Central Valley was "reclaimed" by dams. Sacramento-born Joan Didion wrote of this reclamation in *Where I Was From*, commenting that "the annual reappearance of a marsh that did not drain to the sea until late spring or summer was referred to locally as 'the high water,' . . . and houses were routinely built with raised floors to accommodate it." My own house, built in 1920, is raised, and in Sacramento we still call houses in that style a high-water bungalow, though the high water has long ceased.

Not only was it easy to forget the river was close by, but having a big goal to pursue also spurred me to plan bigger trips to marquee swimming spots, rather than taking an hour for an easy dip. For my twelfth dunk, I had an ambitious plan to head to Chico and hike up a canyon to swimming holes I hadn't visited in years. My oldest friend Sarah and I had been trying to make this happen for a long time, but we'd been smoked out and thwarted by COVID and our busy lives. In 2021, we were determined to make a day of it at some point. On the August day we chose, smoke from the Dixie Fire was holding off. I planned to hit the road at 8:30, but I woke up in the middle of the night with a sore throat. I was vaccinated, but I'd been reading so much about breakthrough infections from the new Delta variant that I got paranoid. I found a rapid testing center (home tests were not yet widely available) and shifted our plan later.

The testing center was makeshift and hard to find, tucked in the back of a parking lot deep in a sketchy neighborhood. My test results didn't come in the promised thirty minutes. Or an hour. By then I had hit the road, assuming results would be negative. As I drove, smoke started smudging the horizon to the north. An hour and a half post-test, I pulled over to call the testing site. No answer. I called Sarah; the heat and smoke had both increased, and we were both worried about infection. We called it off and, glum, I turned around.

As I got back to Sacramento, my results came at last: COVID negative. I was tempted to go home and sulk, but instead I took my book and my camp chair and the lunch I'd packed for my more-fun outing with a dear friend, and I headed to a wading and dipping spot I'd visited before in the tame suburbs of Sacramento, William B. Pond Recreation Area. There's no pond there; rather, the river narrows from wide shallow riffles, splits around an island, and pours over clay outcroppings into a waist-deep hole. Once there, I threw down my stuff in as much shade as I could find on a hundred-degree afternoon and waded in as fast as I could. I was learning that the best cure for an annoying day was to let cool water wash it away, and as I got deeper, I let my feet float up, arched back, and then jackknifed under. A short swim was enough refreshment to settle down for a while. Hair dripping, I set up my chair by a pile of smooth round cobbles.

As wild and scenic as any river may look, almost none of what I saw on my river outings in California was truly wild. Nothing was untouched by European settlement; everything was reshaped by the lust for gold and control over the land. That river rock wasn't native to the area; it was washed far downstream by hydraulic mining done in the late nineteenth century to strip gold from ancient riverbeds and high ground. Later, dams channelized and controlled the rivers, for the sake of agricultural profit and flood prevention. The depth and flow rate of the Lower American and most other rivers I swam in didn't depend on rainfall or snowmelt, at least not directly; instead, it rose and fell based on reservoir management and dam releases. European settlement and profit taking disrupted both natural patterns and Indigenous ecological management, leaving scars on the land that are now so old they seem original. They also left behind place names that reveal their priorities and hierarchies. Gold Rush–era settlements on riverbanks were called "bars," and they were often named for what miners could take, as in Rich Bar, or for the ethnic or other groups that settled there: Mormon Bar, French Bar, Chinese Camp, Spanish Flat, Dutch Flat. One place close to Sacramento was called Negro Bar; now part of a state park, it was renamed Black Miners Bar only in 2022.

At William B. Pond, I alternated between reading my book and swimming when I got too hot, my restless bad mood eased by the burble of the river. An alert crossed my phone screen: another fire start, forty-odd miles to the northeast. On the horizon, the smoke plume bloomed, an unsettling moment of déjà vu. Later, I would learn it was called the River Fire.

The acrid old-ashtray smell of several fires hung in the one-hundred-degree air the next week, too, and one by one, texts rolled in from three friends. Each of them bailed on a long-planned day with our kids at a favorite swimming hole not far from where the River Fire burned. They were wise, and my own kids refused to go, but I was determined. I remembered the feel of a damp mask clinging to my face as I did the backstroke in 2020, during the month of smoke; this air quality was nowhere near that bad. I had to go while the going was possible, if not good.

Again the American River came to my rescue. This time, I headed to the small Gold Rush–era town of Auburn, half an hour from Sacramento and near the confluence of the river's North and Middle Forks. I'd read for years about a massive swimming area upstream from where the forks met, Clark's Hole. Getting there required a trail walk of about three-quarters of a mile. I was late getting out the door, and the sky was yellow gray with smoke by the time I got there. I made a critical error in following the directions I'd found online: there's a bridge by the parking area, and you're supposed to cross the bridge and hike on the trail on the river's east side. I didn't realize that and took a trail on the west side, following the instructions to look for a big blackberry patch and boulders as signs of the correct spur trail to the hole.

At a fork in the trail, I spotted blackberry bushes and a lot of big boulders, so down I went. I failed to consider two facts: first, I hadn't been walking long enough to go that far; second, at most places in the Sierra foothills you can count on finding blackberry bushes and boulders. Also, the slightly widened river at the bottom of the steep trail didn't look anywhere near massive. But I was red and sweaty, a contrast to the water's cool blue appeal, and the trail that continued along the canyon rim was faint, so I convinced myself it was the right place and scrambled down. I was lucky not to get poison oak or take a bad fall on the steep makeshift trail's loose rocks. I had to bend and twist so much to get footholds that my metal water bottle fell out of my backpack's side pocket, clanging over rocks as it bounced. I was struck with fear it might spark; the weeds and brush were so tinder dry I could start a fire of my own. Even the invasive blackberry bushes, tough survivors that can weather almost any drought, were brown and dead, their fruit withered before it could ripen.

Down at the water's edge, it was obvious this was not the real swimming hole: too small, too shallow, too close to the trailhead. It was also obvious that I should not have attempted the non-trail down, and that the way up would be a punishment. I decided to wade upstream, as far as needed. Dogged, I slipped over algae furring the rocks, picking my way through the current and stubbing my toes on the uneven riverbed. (My swimming hobby was bad news for pedicures.)

To get past some small rapids to Clark's, I had to hoist up and over a big rock and wade through a murky shallow before a bend in the river opened up to a winner of a hole: deep and wide as a small lake, the banks punctuated by big jumping rocks swarming with kids. I slid under the water and popped up to backstroke—my favorite way to swim, especially where there's a good view. A mix of oaks and evergreens shimmered in my peripheral vision. High above hung Foresthill Bridge, the tallest bridge in California, built when it seemed this spot would be dammed to form yet another reservoir. There was a long-running controversy over the Auburn Dam, and bumper stickers reading "Build it, dam it!" used to be a common sight around northern California. Construction on the dam halted in 1975, and the gorgeous canyon of the North Fork with its swimming holes and hiking trails was saved.

Just as the Lower American offered easy in-town swims for me, Clark's Hole gave Auburn locals a place to cool off. From the late 1940s to the early 1960s, Auburn's recreation district set it up as a municipal swimming hole, with lifeguards and swimming lessons, changing rooms and a sandy beach. Local papers reported thousands cavorting there during the swimming season of 1949. Now, the setting looks wild except for the wide dirt trail, and the riverbanks are so steep it's hard to picture how sand could be trucked in or where changing rooms might be, but it's one more piece of evidence of how much things evolve. If a river tamed by human intervention could look wild, if forests could heal from fire, if construction on a bad dam could halt, maybe my family could reshape itself around the scar of divorce.

~

My upbringing pushed me toward perfectionism in various subtle ways. My mom suffered severe depression, but even when she was medicated always took the pessimistic view. Despite my dad's penchant for fun, his work ethic was and remains formidable; he had two full-time careers (lawyer and almond grower) and never seemed to feel satisfied at rest. I was a good eldest daughter and people pleaser, and for much of my life, I hadn't realized how I had absorbed their different modes of striving, of never feeling I was working hard enough, and of spurning the sunny outlook. Sometimes a little pessimism—or, as I liked to think of it, realism—served me well, especially in situations like Brad's illness, during which I became an ace in a crisis. But sometimes all my planning led to disappointment and unhappiness.

I'd set an ambitious goal for myself to swim in fifty different places, and in the early days I wanted each one to be a unique, glorious success. Sometimes, as with Jenny Lake or Natural Bridges, I hit the mark. But sometimes, the realities of fire, smoke, heat, drought, and life meant I had to settle for good enough. Some of my dunks were spontaneous, born of pulling over at any promising roadside turnout next to a body of water. Some were hard-won disappointments, or tame submersions in the forks and flow of a no-longer-wild river. It didn't matter. Like life, the 50 Dunks Project was a big container, with room for good enough as well as for the best, and a crummy swim was always better than a day of bickering.

Amid climate change and middle age, I realized that what I most needed was to seize the day, any day, to find what pleasure I could take from life. In a conversation with an acquaintance, I once referred to myself as middle aged, and she protested that I shouldn't say that, that it sounded so old. I laughed and replied that I was in my late forties, and it was a simple fact of math that "middle aged" was the best I could hope for. Either I was in the middle, if I were to live a long time, or I was closer to the end. I was midstream in my life, and it was up to me what I did with the latter part of it; either I could keep pushing against the current, exhausting myself in the process, or I could find an easier, more satisfying flow.

The timing for a lot of my dips, in that fire-ravaged summer of 2021, was terrible. But getting in the water always felt good. Likewise, the timing of contemplating ending my marriage and remaking my life was bad. While Brad's health was stable, he was still chronically ill. Our family was facing turmoil as well; in 2020, his mother had undergone cancer treatment for lymphoma—a different subtype from Brad's, but still a painful reminder of his illness—and she relapsed in August. The confluence of these factors kept me mired in guilt, which in turn led to stagnation. I had dammed up my life; it was up to me to release the flow, in hopes I could return to something a shade freer, a little more like its original shape. In the waters of the American River, I realized that I might have to make the best of bad timing. My happiness couldn't wait six years, and the only time I could get out would have to be the time I made for myself.

CHAPTER FOUR

A RESERVOIR WITH A VIEW

DUNK 14: *Russian River estuary, Jenner*
DUNK 15: *Somewhere in the Sonoma County redwoods*

My lungs tightened, breath coming out in shorter puffs, as I climbed the one-lane road. I wasn't sure where I was headed or if there was anything but forest at its end, but as usual I was hoping to find water. Years before, my grandfather had told me about a spot he used to swim. He said a trail led up to a spring, or a pond, or something, in the redwoods deep in the rural, mystical western hills of Sonoma County, where he spent summers growing up. By the time he was regaling me with stories, he wasn't exactly up for a hike. He had polio as an adult in the 1950s, and his abdominal muscles were paralyzed, leading to a bad back. My memories of the conversation were hazy and confusing. The creeks nearby were mere trickles, and the place he described was too high up to be the nearby Russian River, which winds through the flatlands of Sonoma County before emptying into the ocean at Jenner Beach. At Jenner that morning, I had gone for a dip in the river's salty estuary, but still—always—I wanted another swim.

My family of origin gave me a lot of overt and unspoken training in how to be appropriate, high achieving, and responsible, but less in how to temper obligation with freedom and pleasure. Maybe that's why my grandfather's off-the-cuff mention of the swimming hole echoed in my mind for so long: here was a glimpse of the man I knew as a businessman with a briefcase, or a paterfamilias making a speech before carving the turkey, running free as a kid. I have a picture of him holding a fishing pole, dated 1929, wearing round wire-frame glasses and overalls and a sideways cap, hair flopping in his eyes.

It was that long-ago kid I thought of as I climbed, looking for the trail back to my own pre-striving childhood self. Had I imagined my grandfather's swimming spot? It was one brief, shapeless tale out of many he had told me. Tales of childhood in San Francisco before the bridges were built, of buying sand dabs at Fisherman's Wharf when it was a working dock and not a tourist attraction. Tales of his infant grandfather being left on the priest's doorstep back in a poor village in the hills above Genoa. Tales of both his grandparents leaving for San Francisco from that village, Pian dei Ratti, which translates to Plain of the Rats; you see why they might leave. Tales of them surviving San Francisco's Earthquake and Fire in 1906 and moving into a house in the working-class South of Market district. My grandfather Blair, born in 1921, was raised in that house, and his father, Steve—whom I called Nonno, Italian for grandfather—lived there until his death at ninety-four in 1989. My mom often took us to stay with him in San Francisco; my brother and I slept in a decades-old Murphy bed in a back bedroom that smelled of dust and stale Wrigley's chewing gum and ancient floor wax.

My Italian background comes from only a slice of my mom's ancestry, but it's funny how that fraction dominated family lore. My grandfather was an expansive raconteur, but there was more to it: the Italian side was the most recent, by generations, to immigrate to the US, so stories of the old country were fresher and had the vivid allure of a fairy tale. Was it true that an unknown woman placed my infant great-great-grandfather on the doorstep of the priest's residence, and the priest raised him and chose a surname for him that's unique to our family, and that means "I raised you" in Latin? There was no way to check, and besides, who would want to disprove such an intriguing story?

My maternal grandparents, Blair and Lois, shaped my life in far more ways than handing down family stories. Children of the Depression who grew up without much money, they met at UC Berkeley when it was free and open to any ambitious Californian, married in 1944, and had my mother ten months later, when my grandfather was overseas in the Navy. They were classic members of the Greatest Generation, lifted to prosperity by the rising postwar tide that benefited so many white Americans. After the war, my grandfather first worked for Pillsbury and then started a business as a grain trader in the gritty Central Valley city of Stockton.

I, the oldest granddaughter, dubbed them Grandma and Grandpa Stockton. My jovial grandfather called me "the apple of his eye," and both my grandparents focused attention and expectations on me from birth. My young self both wanted to live up to their good opinion and sensed that my mother often had scant attention to spare for me. I jumped to take on the mantle of being independent, high achieving, and responsible.

I ate up praise for doing what adults liked: writing thank-you notes, reading books, getting perfect attendance and grades.

As I got older, doing what my elders liked turned into a lot of conventional choices that sometimes had the tiniest of rebellious streaks. For college, I rejected the family tradition of Berkeley in favor of a big East Coast private school, Georgetown—though I now think the lefty ferment of Berkeley would have suited me far better. (My disappointed grandfather consoled himself with the fact that Georgetown was Catholic, though I was not religious and had no intention of becoming so.) I dated nice boys and introduced them to my family. I returned to California and chased prestige in a PhD program and got married to another nice boy. In all this outward success, I failed to explore myself or to understand my own desires, or to live according to what I thought I valued. My feminism and socialist beliefs clashed with my need for approval, so I channeled them into writing papers about feminism, class, and sexuality in Victorian literature, getting an advanced degree for my trouble. Keeping my explorations theoretical rather than actual felt like having my cake and eating it too.

Once when I was a teenager at my grandmother's formal holiday table, she told me that if I didn't learn how to hold my fork properly, no nice boy would ever marry me. I shot back that if a boy cared about how I held my fork, I didn't want to marry him anyway. My grandmother raised her eyebrows. I pretended I didn't care, but I changed how I held my fork. At around the same age, my best friend and I had gone to Chico's only art house theater to see the Merchant-Ivory period film *A Room with a View*, a perfect romantic comedy of manners. I was entranced by the teenaged Helena Bonham Carter as well-to-do heroine Lucy Honeychurch, trained to propriety and expected to marry well. She travels to Italy with her prim chaperone (played by Dame Maggie Smith); there, a poorer young man, George Emerson, awakens her passionate streak with a kiss in a field of poppies. At my grandmother's table, I felt like Lucy at the film's outset, uneasily straining for an unknown freedom, but bound by expectations.

~

Brad, the girls, and I were in the redwoods for his birthday. Exactly a year before, in mid-August 2020, we'd been in peaceful Sonoma County during a vicious heat wave, unusual for the cool coastal region, which turned into the dry lightning storms that sparked dozens of wildfires. I felt a little superstitious about the anniversary. It seemed like every fire season was worse than the last, and even high in the damp redwoods it was tinder dry.

Most of the rivers I love in California flow to the San Francisco Bay. My favorite exception is the Russian River, whose short course drains and often floods a bucolic 1,500-square-mile watershed north of the Bay Area. Named for a short-lived nineteenth-century Russian colony of fur trappers and traders, the Russian River region is best known outside California for its pinot noirs. Past famous vineyards near Healdsburg and Forestville, the river flattens and widens through modest vacation communities, rising quickly to inundate them in wet years. Near the dilapidated small town of Monte Rio, the river passes Bohemian Grove, an infamous all-male, not-so-secret summer camp run by San Francisco's exclusive Bohemian Club for Republican old money and power brokers. My grandfather spoke reverently of the Bohemian Club, and I always sensed he wished he'd amassed enough money and influence to be invited to join. The very idea of Bohemian Grove, with past attendees like Ronald Reagan and George H. W. Bush, feels out of place in the otherwise hippie-influenced region that locals call West County.

Monte Rio also boasts a Quonset hut movie theater with a perpetual FOR SALE sign, a long-shuttered bar called the Pink Elephant that my grandma and friends used to drop into on a lark, and a rocky river beach my family has visited for years. I've often seen the beach packed, but in this drought year the water was low and mucky. Even from the bridge, I could see florid yellow-green bloom. I'm not fussy about river water, but it looked too gross even for me, and I crossed the river off my list for a swim.

Algae aside, the whole area has a feeling of secret enchantment—not fake rituals for conservative men, but the quieter magic of sun slanting through redwoods, cool misty mornings where the fog burns off slowly, decrepit little summer cottages on stilts, rolling hills and quaint surprises: farms selling the fragrant Gravenstein apples my grandmother used to bake into pies, a stellar bakery so popular it runs out of bread daily, a drive-through pottery stand selling clay sea creatures on the honor system. I had my favorites of these attractions, rituals developed over years of visiting the area with Brad and the girls. Although the four of us were all together on that 2021 trip, I have no memory of my interactions with Brad.

The morning of my climb to seek my grandfather's swimming hole, the four of us had taken a drive to Goat Rock State Beach, where the Russian River empties into the sea and where the riptides are among the deadliest in California. It also hosts a colony of harbor seals, and signs warn against bothering them or their young. The river curves in a wide S through ever-shifting sand dunes, and sometimes its narrow outlet to the open ocean is sealed off by drifting sand. The beach is almost always cold, as northern California beaches are. Visits there are tied up with my early memories, and now with my daughters' as well. I have a picture of my mom camping there with my dad, before I was born, wearing a navy blue puffer jacket and looking like my older daughter's twin. Other faded photos show me and an aunt and uncle, and my mom and grandparents, huddled over a picnic in the wind. On this foggy August day, my daughters posed for pictures on a big driftwood log, hugging each other for warmth, and I lay back on the same log to take a selfie, but we skipped any family pictures.

The girls bickered and wrestled on the log as I walked off alone. I saw an opportunity for a dunk; the ocean may be dangerous, but the estuary, sheltered by its long sand spit, is calm and bracing. Pelicans flapped through the white sky as I waded hip deep, the cold prickling my legs. As I was mulling going under, I felt the odd sense of eyes on me. It was a speckled harbor seal, gazing at me. Its eyes and demeanor were as friendly as a wet Australian cattle dog. I went under once, twice, and a third time in the brine. When I surfaced, refreshed, the seal was gone, but a little farther away a black one bobbed, a kindred aquatic creature that seemed to recognize me as a kind of selkie. Their serene presence somehow eased the loneliness of my unraveling marriage.

That afternoon, I pored over a topo map and Google Maps. Both showed a set of springs and, nearby, an unnamed oblong patch of blue. Any roads ended well before the blue patch, but I thought if I followed the street that ended closest to the water, I might find a trail. I asked the girls if they wanted to come. Nora had flopped face down for a nap; Lucy looked up from her phone long enough to say no. I suppressed nagging thoughts of wondering what it had all been for: the work, the sleepless nights, the endless culling of outgrown clothes and toys, the thousands of weeknight dinners.

Part of me knew that was the frustration of raising adolescents, but part of me felt like a sucker, cheated of the family happiness that doing all the right things was supposed to bring me. I had followed the rules like a good older daughter, like a granddaughter whose grandparents loved to brag. I had not let anything go down on my permanent record. I had worn a white dress and veil and smiled for family photos and earned degrees and written hundreds, maybe thousands, of thank-you notes, and here I was, unfulfilled. My grandparents were dead, and so was my mom, and their approval couldn't last me a lifetime. I needed satisfaction that came from my real insides, not from outward expectations that I'd internalized. I understood that intellectually, but I struggled to put it into practice.

Tree roots cracked the single-lane road heading uphill, and its crumbling asphalt overhung the deep canyon. I kept an ear out for cars; the roads were barely wide enough for a single car, but traffic was two way. As I climbed, I marveled at the idea that someone had looked at these gorges and the mighty trees and thought it would be a great place to harvest timber and build tiny houses. How did humans do this much work, I wondered, in the days before bulldozers? First, in the late nineteenth century, the area was logged. Then, as author and area resident Manjula Martin writes in *The Last Fire Season*, "the newly minted logger baron began marketing the land as a camp, a summer-cabin enclave for San Francisco residents, who could take a brisk four-hour train ride to an idyllic forest setting that, as a newspaper ad for the development boasted, 'favorably compares with Switzerland and our own Yosemite.' In truth, the sylvan hill was only about one thousand feet high (Yosemite's peaks were closer to ten thousand) . . . but the trees were majestic. And the cabins were cheap: $20 each." They were, in short, priced for even working-class San Franciscans, back in the day when a working-class job paid a living wage.

The great-grandfather I called Nonno worked for the telephone company collecting bills door-to-door. An old family story tells of him going to the home of Italian speakers to collect and, time after time, hearing them cursing him in Italian, until one day he finally replied in the language, to their embarrassment. My great-grandparents first went to the redwoods for the summer in 1919, after Nonno returned from infantry service during World War I. Into the 1960s, this region had the vibe of an old-time family summer resort, like a Western version of the Poconos or the Catskills (for which my main frame of reference was *Dirty Dancing*). In place of the clubhouse and Saturday night dances my mom remembered from the 1950s now stood a rusting swing set, a trailer housing a post office, and a volunteer fire department, which blows a World War II–era siren to summon firefighters in any emergency. It echoes up the ferny canyons of several unnamed seasonal rills, which are mere trickles or entirely dry in summer. One of them, I reasoned, had to lead to its source, but I had no idea of the way up.

Then I caught a break. Coming down the hill was a family group, the mom loaded up with a beach bag, dogs wet and muddy, and a gaggle of swimsuit-wearing little kids with long hair in damp clumps, carrying ratty towels. The kids reminded me of my own girls, when they were littler and I could simply make them join me on river outings. Any hike came with complaints, but also with smiles for cute photos and the whoops of jumping in. I had a keen sense of childhoods ending, of a change coming. I was hiking up the road alone; the woman leading the ragtag young group might not read me as a fellow mom, a member of the frazzled sorority that gives each other subtle I'm-so-tired nods of recognition. I was an independent agent, no story attached to me. But her presence opened the possibility that I could write one.

The dogs bounded up to me, and when the mom called them off, I shot my shot.

"Hey! Do you mind my asking where you guys have been? I heard there was a place to swim somewhere up here, but I don't know where it is," I said, gesturing at the kids' suits.

"Oh, we were up at the reservoir," she said. This was promising. I tried to act casual.

"Oh? How do you get there?" I asked.

"There's a trail off to the right up a ways," she said. "It's on private property, so it's roped off."

"So . . . can you not go?" I asked. I had no intention of not going, but I wanted to know what level of trespassing I was letting myself in for.

She shrugged. "Meh . . . everyone does. It's an easy trail to follow. Just follow the creek and you'll find it."

Her pointers led me to a NO TRESPASSING sign on a chain strung between two trees. Someone less rule-following than I had painted over the words, but even my good-girl self was willing to duck under the chain. A dirt trail wound through gnarled oaks and bracken, high above a creek bed. The sharp, spicy scent of California bay overpowered the must of dry leaves. The only sign of other people was the existence of the trail. I had followed it and the creek for maybe half an hour when I came to a bare-dirt slope, topped by an embankment. Splashes and voices rang through the woods.

At the top, I found a long, skinny pond with a straight line of piled earth at its eastern end, clearly human made. The word "reservoir" suggests concrete dams and unnatural spaces; in droughty California, it also evokes low water and the grand-scale bathtub rings of exposed lakebeds. This water looked nothing like that. It was a deep, cloudy jade, like an oversized pendant my grandmother had bought in Hong Kong, surrounded by reeds and bushes and thick redwoods that grew right down to the muddy edge. At the far end there was a green bloom and a fallen tree, but in the middle the water looked clean. The sun had slanted lower in the sky, and its glow, caught between summer's glare and fall's golden bath, rippled on the surface. Although there were one or two other swimmers, I felt the peace and completeness of solitude, not the ache of loneliness.

The California landscape looks very different from Surrey, but the unexpected, peaceful water in thick woods reminded me of a pivotal scene in *A Room with a View*. Lucy and her priggish fiancé Cecil Vyse (Daniel Day-Lewis, playing hard against type) escape their boring engagement party. She wears exquisite white lace; he has a stiff straw boater and lorgnette; they struggle to make conversation, and he says plaintively that he thinks she feels more at home with him in a room than in the countryside. She replies, casually devastating, "When I *do* think of you, it is always in a room."

Lucy says that her family calls the pond the Sacred Lake and that her brother Freddy loves to bathe there. "And you?" Cecil asks.

"I used to bathe here, too," says Lucy, "until I was found out."

Cecil then asks to kiss her—for the first time, although they're engaged. The kiss is awkward, fumbling; he pecks at her lips, whereas she, schooled by her Italian kiss, goes in for something more passionate, knocking down Cecil's eyepiece. The film depicts many moments in which Lucy realizes Cecil and his conventional life are wrong for her, but this one, emphasizing her pent-up and objectless passion, is among the most poignant.

The tragedy of the indoorsy Cecil becomes even keener in the movie's second Sacred Lake scene, a joyful farce that imprinted on my fourteen-year-old memory. Unaware of George and Lucy's fling, Lucy's brother Freddy has befriended George Emerson, inviting him to "come and have a bathe!" They and the local vicar are cavorting—splashing, shouting, and full-frontal naked, to my young self's shock and delight—when Lucy, Cecil, and her mother come strolling. Free-spirited George jumps into the path, dick swinging, howling, beating his chest, as Lucy tries to suppress her laughs and Cecil recoils. This is the beginning of the end: Lucy calls off the engagement. By the movie's end, she has eloped with George, and the final scene shows Lucy and George sitting in a window of the hotel where the movie began, a view of Florence in the background, George kissing her ardently.

A Room with a View was formative for me, but I understand Lucy's resistance to and her eventual choice of freedom now far better than I understood it as a teen. The strictures around class, propriety, and money were vastly different for me growing up in late-twentieth-century California than in Edwardian England, but they have some parallels. Lucy was to come into her inheritance upon marriage, but when she marries George, Freddy threatens to withhold it. My own inheritance set me free, but it took me years to appreciate that freedom.

By the modest standards of my hometown, my nuclear family was comfortably upper-middle class. My grandparents, however, had become wealthy, thanks to my grandfather's business thriving and his college pals including him in investment groups. My grandparents were so vibrant, traveling into their seventies, that I hardly thought their wealth would affect my future. But it came to me earlier than I could have imagined. My grandfather died in 2007, and my mother—distressed by both grief and the money she inherited—was never quite stable again. In the grips of a profound depressive episode, she took her life at the age of sixty-four. Mourning her suicide and coping with its inheritance, in all senses, swamped me for years. That inheritance, however, has enabled everything about my life now, including the creative life that led me to write this book and funded the necessary time and travel. The writing and publishing industry is full of such privilege, but we rarely discuss it, much less how who can afford to tell their own stories shapes the broader cultural discourse. As a white woman in my fifties, I am a member of the dominant group of storytellers, those afforded the privilege of examining our own lives, something I'm conscious of as I write about finding pleasure and space. As a freelance writer in my thirties, I was always hustling for whatever work paid; after my mom died, I was freed to write essays, creative nonfiction, and eventually my first book. My inheritance was also a crucial cushion during the years of Brad's cancer. There was a long time when neither of us could work, he because of illness, I because of the demands of caring for him and our children. It was a profound and guilty luxury that at that time we had savings and a guaranteed income that outstripped his salary and my writing income combined.

At the reservoir, I relied on a different inheritance, that of memory, as I kicked off my hiking sandals and slid into the fresh, silky water. It bubbled into my ears as I dove under, muffling the other swimmers, who were playing and splashing like the men at the Sacred Lake. The sun sank lower through a light haze, and I backstroked lazy laps, gazing at the blue expanse fringed by spiky black redwoods, while I waited for them to leave. When they did, I stripped off my swimsuit, tossed it to the bank with a wet thud, and floated for a magical few minutes. I didn't stay much longer. It was getting toward dinnertime, and I still felt bound enough by convention that I didn't want to be caught swimming naked, though how much I cared about that was starting to change.

Grabbing a tree root, I hoisted myself out of the water for the most uncomfortable part of any swim. Getting out meant wriggling back into resistant wet clothes as they bunched and twisted, attempting to rinse the dirt off each foot without getting more on the other foot, shaking water out of tangled hair. I was getting hungry, so I picked a few blackberries hanging over the pond, their tart juice staining my tongue. My husband and children must be getting hungry too. I needed to get going, but I turned to take one more look at the mirror of sun and ferns and trees.

Was this the place my grandfather had swum nearly one hundred years ago? If so, did he take this trail? In the eight or nine decades since he explored in his Coke-bottle glasses and street-urchin overalls, the trails and the woods had likely changed. Maybe his way up was now covered with poison oak or overgrown with redwoods. There were no topo map quarter sections, no Google Maps in his day, no satellite view to find water, but I'd be willing to bet he probably found his way much as I did: spotting wet kids and getting a nudge in the right direction.

In the end, I hadn't needed my grandfather's instructions. I didn't even need to know if this was his swimming spot. I've poked around looking for the history of the reservoir and learned that it used to provide the drinking water for the vacation homes downhill, but I couldn't find when it was constructed. It doesn't matter, just as it doesn't matter whether my great-great-grandfather was really a foundling raised by a priest. I was still connected to the reservoir of family stories and support that shaped my life but also sent me down trails that were not my true path.

Not long before he died, my grandfather sat me down to talk about his money. He and my grandmother had used it to enjoy themselves, he said, and he hoped that someday when I was able to take a trip or do something I couldn't otherwise afford, that I would think of them. I do think of them and of that conversation almost every day. My gratitude to them is beyond what any thank-you note could convey. Yet I also had to overcome an unspoken emotional inheritance. I chose safety, stability, and conventionality in my youth, and my grandparents were proud. Though they were long dead as I wrestled with whether to leave my marriage, their expectations and approval still made a guilty echo in my mind, even as their money meant I could afford to leave. I did not need to fear that an unsuitable marriage, or leaving one, would endanger my inheritance. I could flash further back in Lucy Honeychurch's story than her choice between a dull prig and free spirit. I could choose to swim whether I got found out or not.

CHAPTER FIVE

A RECHARGED AQUIFER

DUNK 16: *Edwards Crossing, South Yuba River*
DUNK 18: *Monterey Bay*
DUNK 19: *San Lorenzo River*
DUNK 20: *Barton Springs, Austin, Texas*

The sky was a hazy yellow gray, the AQI was a "very unhealthy" three hundred, and it was one hundred degrees as I loaded my car with an overnight bag and a hopeful last-minute tote holding a swimsuit, towel, and water sandals. It was August 29, 2021, and summer's heat wasn't fading. The Dixie Fire still raged on, but on that day, the evacuation order for Jonesville was lifted at last. Our cabin had made it through. I wasn't headed there, though; rather, I was leaving my suffocating home for a hotel ballroom in the small Gold Rush–era town of Grass Valley. A caregiver-support nonprofit had invited me to speak, offering an overnight stay in lieu of a speaker's fee. I had an unusual amount of solo travel that fall, thanks to such invitations. When I was asked to speak, I looked up nearby rivers and lakes in hopes of finding a good dunk nearby.

The irony of giving talks about the biggest strain on my marriage when I wanted to end it was not lost on me. I felt like a secret fraud talking about caring for my husband whenever a Q&A led to the awkward, predictable inquiry, "And how are you and your husband doing now?" I never lied, but I also never said we were on the brink of divorce, afraid of the audience's judgment. Instead, I yammered about how much the care relationship had changed the marriage. A flush of shame and fear ran through me as I thought ahead to a time when the answer might be "Actually, we're separated."

Grass Valley is a few miles from my favorite swimming river, the South Yuba, which boasts a string of emerald-green, pristine pools—the reason I said yes to the overnight there. When I saw the smoke and weather, I considered turning around and driving home after the talk. The ragged last few days of summer always felt busy, and school would start later that week. After my afternoon talk, however, the smoke was clearing. I sprawled on the hotel bed, enjoyed the lack of demands on me, and slept hard. Pristine blue skies surprised me the next morning, and I headed out early for my sixteenth dunk, aiming for a century-old bridge and a short hike to a waterfall I'd read about in a swimming hole guide. On a flat boulder below the bridge, a rangy naked couple bowed in sun salutations; locals accept the remote parts of the river as clothing optional. A mile down the trail, a small feeder creek spouted some ten feet over an overhang, with room to stand behind the waterfall. I peeled my backpack off sweaty shoulders and let the thunderous cascade pound my traps and tangle my hair before I jumped in the wider river below. Nobody was around, so I stripped down like the couple on the rock, letting the river rinse my self-consciousness away—though not all of it. I wasn't up for doing sun salutations.

As I picked my way back upriver, I slithered into every deep green pool and lay in the sun on boulders, their smooth granite heft warming my skin and giving off a mineral scent. Once or twice I caught the faintest whiff of smoke and looked for clouds boiling up, but I saw no fire starts. I lost track of time watching iridescent trout flash by many feet deep. The fish, the waterfall, the sunny day: all reminded me that even in catastrophe we can still find oases of pleasure. Smoke settled as I drove home, where the oppressive sense of climate and family doom closed back in. But I was grateful for my brief luck.

Prioritizing my own work and travel for it felt both uncomfortable and exhilarating. I'd stopped or downshifted my career as a writer so many times: when I quit a dream food-editor job to follow Brad to Sacramento, after the birth of each of our daughters, to cope with grief and the responsibilities of managing the estate following my mother's suicide, again when Brad fell ill. Each time my career took two steps back for a care responsibility, I struggled to take a step forward. I always felt I was losing ground as a writer, a thinker, a human being. Instead, I felt like I was solely what feminist philosopher Kate Manne calls a "*human giver*, a woman who is held to owe many if not most of her distinctively human capacities to a suitable boy or man, ideally, and his children."

With my new book and increasing work, I felt like I was coming back to my professional self. Work travel was also a way to squeeze in my 50 Dunks Project; with about a year left, I had thirty-four swims to go, meaning I would need to average one about every ten days. On one road trip to Monterey to give a keynote on caregiving, I snuck into the rough water of Monterey Bay across from the conference hotel; the next day, I detoured to the woods near Santa Cruz on the way home for a fifty-five-degree swim in the San Lorenzo River, in a pool misnamed the Garden of Eden. I hit traffic, got home late, and felt guilty as I so often did when I traveled, though Brad was mostly tolerant of my absence. He had taken a disability retirement, and he had recovered enough to take care of the girls, who needed less hands-on care by then. Nora was starting her junior year of high school and had her driver's license, and Lucy was entering seventh grade. Brad did, however, have his own travel and care responsibilities that fall, flying back and forth to Canada to help his parents during his mother's treatment.

It felt like we were easing into separate lives. By then, it seemed like our only remaining point of connection, besides parenting, was writing. Yet I'd long had a buried feeling that what seemed like a bond—intellectual and creative work—was pushing us apart. Brad had always seemed willing to accommodate my work—if it didn't clash with his. When the girls were younger and I was a full-time freelance writer, if a kid got sick, I was almost always the one to cancel or shift work obligations to be home with them. If I protested, he said he couldn't cancel class. He could, of course, thanks to the job security of tenure and considerable freedom of academic work. He chose to inconvenience my work rather than his own and refused to acknowledge that that was a choice, even though he got paid whether he held class or not and I did not get paid if I missed an assignment. I knew, too, that if I missed enough of them to seem unreliable, which I never did, I would stop getting assignments. Although our work contributed almost equally to the household income, I sensed that deep down, maybe even unconsciously, he felt his was the real work, and mine was optional.

When Brad was working, I resented his professional freedom while I struggled to fit in my work around doing the bulk of household labor. Now he was retired, but was still writing, including poetry and a yearslong academic project on *Hamlet*. In one fight I told him that if he were a tenth as curious about me as he was about the subject of his book, our marriage wouldn't be in trouble. While he delved into Latin texts, I still did most of what it took to keep the family running and tried to write. I was meeting with more real-world success than I'd ever enjoyed: a new book, articles in such outlets as the *New York Times* and *TIME*, well-paid speaking engagements that came with travel to Connecticut and Texas. Ironically, just when things were going well, I felt burned out by my book launch and the long string of personal crises that led to it. I knew I should be writing more about caregiving in support of the book, but could muster little to say. The only writing that sparked my interest were the short, casual blog posts I jotted down about my swims.

A recent crop of divorce memoirs and autofiction looks at the gendered strains involved when two creative people make a life together: Leslie Jamison's *Splinters*, Sarah Manguso's *Liars*, Miranda July's *All Fours*, Maggie Smith's *You Could Make This Place Beautiful*, and more. Smith's lyrical vignettes describe leaving for work trips after her poem "Good Bones" went viral. Her surprising success as a poet sparks creative envy from her husband, whom she had met in a writing program. Before they separate, Smith's husband introduces her at a reading for her second book and says "many kind things." Smith thinks, "Huh.

What he said about me and my writing in public felt different than his attitude at home." My own mom did part-time contract work but handled most of the home front, and I nodded at Smith's frustration at how much her life resembled her own mother's: "I saw myself and my husband as different—more progressive, more equal in our household, both with graduate degrees, both respected in our fields—but were we? The division of labor in our home told a different story." In the same vignette, Smith writes that when she traveled, "I didn't feel missed as a person. I felt missed as staff. My invisible labor was made painfully visible when I left the house."

Many Gen-X and younger women have written of similar reckonings, and of their dissatisfaction—which I share—with the limited victories of past decades' have-it-all, lean-in feminism. The time women spend on the housework "second shift," as influential sociologist Arlie Hochschild dubbed it, did decline relative to their male partners' contributions up until the 1980s, but progress on equality in the home has since stopped, resulting in what Paula England called a "stalled and uneven" gender revolution. In the recent *What's On Her Mind*, sociologist Alison Daminger sums up the shift in hands-on household labor: "we see a period of rapid change coinciding with women's mass entry into the paid labor force, followed by a long plateau in which gender convergence trickles off or stops altogether." Her book argues, however, that the gendered revolution in cognitive labor—the infamous mental load—has "barely started."

Sarah Manguso's novel *Liars* offers a thinly fictionalized version of this dynamic, on which she commented sharply in an interview in *Alta*, responding to a question about Gen-X women growing up believing they were "finally free from the confines of the home" in the wake of *Roe v. Wade* and second-wave feminism. "'The women of my generation were sold a bill of goods for a new kind of heterosexual partnership that, for most of us, never really materialized,' [Manguso] says." Similarly, the author Ada Calhoun writes: "For my entire adult life, I'd dedicated myself to being kind, patient, and supportive. . . . In love, as in work, I'd taken pride in being low maintenance and low needs. Throughout my 15 years of marriage, I'd handled the lion's share of logistics and made most of the money. But in my mid-40s, I realized that the reward for being ultra-responsible isn't a gold star. Rather, it was even more responsibility."

Calhoun also shared my fear of judgment because of past public writing about marriage: "Getting divorced felt very off-brand. I'd written a whole book . . . about finding ways to stay together." In *Already Toast*, I wrote that when caregiving was at its hardest, I often wanted to run away, but I had stayed. Now my book itself held me back from changing my life; the thought of promoting a book about caring for my husband while explaining that he wasn't my husband anymore felt too embarrassing to contemplate.

Despite those lingering qualms, I was not only increasingly admitting to myself that I wanted to end my marriage but starting to believe a large part of the problem was marriage itself. I was far from alone. According to a 2015 study, women initiate nearly 70 percent of divorces in heterosexual marriages, a number that rises to 90 percent when the women are college educated. It's not just that women are dissatisfied in relationships with men. As the author of the study, Michael Rosenfeld, said, "'I assumed, and I think other scholars assumed, that women's role in breakups was an essential attribute of heterosexual relationships, but it turns out that women's role in initiating breakups is unique to heterosexual marriage." He posits that marriage is more oppressive than nonmarital heterosexual relationships: "Marriage as an institution has been a little bit slow to catch up with expectations for gender equality."

I would argue that it hasn't just been slow. Rather, it's impossible for marriage to become egalitarian because it is an instrument of patriarchy. I of all people should have known that going in. I wrote my doctoral dissertation about marriage in Victorian Britain, when the legal doctrine of coverture still held (meaning that a married woman's legal identity was subsumed under that of her husband), when married women could not own property but could be abused and raped by their husbands at will, and when divorce required a literal Act of Parliament. Why, exactly, was I so eager to marry as a young feminist in the 1990s, when the backlash against women's rights that runs rampant today was beginning to ferment? Somehow, I didn't connect that history to my own marriage on the cusp of the new millennium. After all, I kept my name, and if anyone asked, Brad would have said he was a feminist; wouldn't that be enough?

If I thought about it at all, with the arrogance of youth, I assumed love and our individual choices could conquer a centuries-old patriarchal structure. More jaded now, I see it as Lyz Lenz does in her blistering *This American Ex-Wife*: "It is possible to have a happy and equal marriage inside an unequal system. But the system itself will always subsume the female partner. I had economic stability, a home, and children, but the cost had been my entire loss of self." Similarly, the recent book *Mad Wife* recounts the pseudonymous author Kate Hamilton's marriage to and divorce from an emotionally abusive man who sexually coerces her. Hamilton is an English professor and a feminist, and although her marriage was far worse than mine, some of the dynamics and her initial naivete rang familiar: "as a woman in a society that pretends equality, married to a man who professed to believe in a marriage of equals without having any idea what that really meant, being married was like living in a cage that no one else could see," she writes. "I was taught by our culture's faux feminism to expect things . . . that I would be routinely denied while being told I was fulfilled."

~

For all my disillusionment with marriage, I couldn't end mine cleanly. I spoke often to my therapist about wanting to leave gracefully, to avoid conflict or bitterness, but I feared the pain of untwisting our tangled lives, the more so since we were so poor at conflict resolution. As a result, Brad and I soldiered on to couples counseling long past when we should have called it quits. Our marriage left so many defeated couples counselors in its wake that I sometimes joke the therapists of greater Sacramento probably have drinks nights to commiserate about us. Despite all the I-statements they taught us to use, nobody helped us communicate much better, much less recover our affection and connection. Over years of painful sessions, thousands of dollars, countless sodden Kleenexes, and many gray love seats we hunched at opposite ends of, I started to doubt the entire project of couples therapy. The therapist works for the relationship, not for either member of it. There's a conflict of interest: the therapist gets paid only if you keep coming back.

Writer Scaachi Koul, who with her husband saw five couples therapists before they split, reports a similar feeling: "Even the ones who seemed to know we were doomed still opened their calendars at the end of each session and urged us to come back, to try again."

Even if we concede that most therapists are well intentioned and not unethically prolonging unsafe or bad relationships, the basic problem remains: the happiness or satisfaction of the individuals in a relationship is not the therapy's focus. Instead, it prioritizes whether the relationship continues to limp along. And there's no hope if partners are incurious about the other person's experience, or the couple can't find common ground in how they communicate or show affection.

One counselor we saw used EFT (emotionally focused therapy). In a typical session, she'd ask us to turn toward each other and share how we felt. I would talk and talk, pouring out my pain at how unseen and taken for granted I felt.

"How do you feel about what Kate said, Brad?" the therapist would say.

"I think . . ." he always started, the words grating on me. The therapist had asked how he felt, but it seemed he only intellectualized, never expressed emotions. He would then go on to analyze whatever I'd said in a way that, to my mind, bore little relationship to what I hoped to communicate.

I'm sure he felt equally misunderstood. He often said he was "trying" as hard as he could. I couldn't understand what he meant; our efforts were invisible to each other. Recalling our fruitless couples therapy now forces me to confront our mutual culpability: while I was busy complaining about how much he didn't care about my feelings, I also wasn't prioritizing his, even though I cared *for* him for years. I'd become attuned to his moods and wishes, in a way both gendered and conditioned by growing up with a mother whose mental state I'd had to discern from a young age, but those years of caring for him had worn me out, and my compassion fatigue increased when I felt no care directed back at me.

In *Splinters*, Leslie Jamison writes: "One of the sly reveals of couples therapy was that each way I found our marriage difficult—which I'd imagined as my own specialized arenas of suffering—actually had its own corollary, like a lost twin, in his experience. I felt like I was always walking on eggshells; so did he. 'Each of you is working so hard in your own separate corners,' our therapist said. 'Each of you feels like you are doing everything.'" For Jamison, this revelation upset her narrative of the marriage. Brad's statements that he was trying as hard as he could to please me drove me only further away. How could he be trying so hard if I couldn't feel it at all? How could he not hear me when I said those attempts were not reaching me? We always missed each other.

At one therapist's suggestion, we set up a joint Google document of notes to tell each other how we were feeling and write about our connection. Although this method gave us a useful pause before we could get heated in verbal communication, I thought it replicated a bigger problem: our relationship was all thinking, no feeling. Sometimes when we did fight, Brad would write a poem processing it and hand it to me, with the intent that I could better understand his feelings or his position. To be clear, these were not love poems, and they were not always straightforward; they required me to study and interpret them. Despite or maybe because of my training in literary interpretation, I was uninterested in conducting a relationship by these means.

At one desperate point I gave him a list of things he could do to make me feel more cared for: buy me flowers occasionally; give me spontaneous hugs; tell me I looked nice sometimes. This resulted in a few stilted side hugs in the kitchen and an automated flower delivery from an online retailer every three weeks. When I traveled, he often forgot to change the order, so sometimes I came home to dead flowers. He was baffled that I didn't find this automated delivery satisfying. He had done the thing I asked! I was shocked that he—an actual professor of English literature, trained in interpreting symbols!—couldn't see that it was never about the flowers, but about him thinking about me when, say, he happened to be in a grocery store passing the flower department, and acting on that thought in a way that he knew would please me, because I had told him it would. But it seemed to me that he never thought about me at all as a person with an inner life, just as the thing supporting all his needs.

That sense extended to our frozen physical relationship. At the time of the pandemic shutdown, we'd been trying to revive our sex life; I was secretly relieved when having the kids home all the time made that impossible. Brad's body was a site of trauma for him, and of some secondary trauma for me. He had gone through things most people would never have survived, and I had been there seeing him suffer for all of it, from holding his hand as a trembling med student stitched his eyelids shut to seeing his elbows bleed from pressure on rough plastic armrests as he hunched on a commode, day after day, because of the gastrointestinal complications of his transplant.

It was all but impossible for his body to recover from that and become a site of pleasure, and it was all but impossible for me to flip a switch back to seeing that body as a source of pleasure, or a site of desire. My shame that I couldn't revert to our prior sexual relationship was tempered when my therapist gently said it wasn't my fault that I couldn't will away aversion forged in horrific hospital days; disgust, she said, is a core emotion. Likewise, it wasn't his fault that his body had become a site of pain, even torture.

My therapist had also recommended a couples counselor specializing in sex and intimacy issues. Our work with him was a long slow-motion disaster. The counselor gave us awkward homework assignments and suggested we read a book called *The Art of Receiving and Giving*, which gave me insight into subtle ways that I'd felt pressured to perform physical intimacy. In one session I said, as gingerly and gently as I could, that I had long felt starved for touch in our relationship, and subtly pressured by the feeling that anytime we touched, there was an unspoken expectation—one I felt unable to question or discuss—that that touch would lead to intercourse. Brad responded with outrage: "So you're saying I'm a rapist?"

I most certainly was not saying that. What I tried to say was that our relationship comprised many unspoken dynamics and unmet needs, and that those were more influenced by patriarchal expectations than I'd understood. As Kate Hamilton puts it in *Mad Wife*, "Marriage . . . trains women to erase ourselves altogether by teaching us that we owe more than the external things owed by men—money, labor, houses. Women owe all our intimacy—our care and emotional investment, the insides of our bodies." While I never felt violated in the same way Hamilton did, I desired a relationship without the subtle sense of entitlement to and movement toward sex when I was lucky enough to be touched. I was twenty-three when Brad and I met, so young that I didn't know myself, and I had accepted the silent terms of our relationship without understanding my need for physicality in all registers, from hugs and hand holding to vigorous exercise or the sense-tingling embrace of flowing water. My 50 Dunks Project was part of a reawakening that was bringing me back into my body, one swim at a time, and it was something my husband and I didn't and couldn't share. He moved deeper into intellectualism and *Hamlet*, I into nature outings and water, as we grew farther apart.

During the pandemic our sessions with the intimacy counselor moved to Zoom, and I often felt like we were merely fighting in front of him on a computer screen. In one of our last sessions, Brad spat bitterly at me: "I got sick, and you're throwing me away." The accusation felt as unfair as a sucker punch. It had been more than five years since his transplant, and he no longer needed a caretaker. I'd stood by him through crisis after crisis. I was not throwing him away because he was sick; I wanted something different from life than what he had to give. I wanted to end our marriage because it didn't feel like a partnership, and he had never given me the emotional support I craved, especially in the wake of my mother's death. I prolonged the agony of the marriage's end because I was so afraid that everyone else would think the same thing Brad did.

In that same session, Brad said I held all the power in the relationship: I ran our lives, I had more money, I was not chronically ill. But there is more than one kind of power. Brad had the subtle power of making me feel unseen and taken for granted, withholding emotional intimacy, and playing on my guilt. "A patriarchal culture such as ours, in which men are taught to exert their will and women are taught to give, to accommodate, to caretake, and to submit, weaponizes male entitlement while normalizing it," writes Kate Hamilton. "Marriage compounds these inequities. In any long-term heterosexual relationship, male entitlement and the power that accompanies it can accrue invisibly over years." Sarah Manguso sums it up bitterly in *Liars*: "A husband might be nothing but a bottomless pit of entitlement. You can throw all your love and energy and attention down into it, and the hole will never fill."

I insisted we quit that therapist. Brad wanted to find another, the right therapist this time, the one who could fix us. I was no longer willing to engage with traditional couples therapy; to me, it felt like endless emotional work for me that produced no change. I read about a different model, discernment therapy, in which the counselor meets with each member of the couple separately, then together. Then come a limited number of sessions that are supposed to lead to a joint decision: stay together or separate. That structure appealed to me. I wanted an authority to look at our fraught marriage and tell us to call it quits, but that's not how couples therapy works.

~

A couples therapist may not outright advise ending a marriage no matter how much they can see you struggling, but a friend sure will. I had a chorus of close friends encouraging me as I dithered over ending things with Brad. I gravitated toward women who had ended their marriages, who could show me a glimpse of a fulfilled life on the other side. My friend Amy, mother of my older daughter's best friend, had been going through a split when we met, when our daughters were in preschool. Now, having long since moved on, she wryly called divorce "our greatest institution." I hoped she was right.

The long stasis of the pandemic, with nothing to look forward to and nowhere to go, had added to my stuck feeling in my marriage. Now, however, I could see friends again, and I could travel. My dunks and the work travel of that fall were waking me up, giving me something to anticipate. My trips became time to come back to the self I was before children, before grief, before care responsibilities. The first post-pandemic flight I took was to Connecticut, where one of my best friends from graduate school had invited me to read at the university she taught at. She knew me before Brad and I met, and we had been roommates and attended each other's weddings, but distance meant we had seen each other seldom in the intervening years. As the cliché goes, though, when we started talking, it felt like no time had passed.

She told me about her and her husband's big project: an ambitious goal of hiking every mile of maintained trails in Connecticut together. I could scarcely imagine that kind of camaraderie, but I envied it—not the hiking per se, but what it showed about what marriage could be. So did her casual mentions of ways her husband cared for her: cups of tea, dinner on the table, shared gardening and home repair projects around their colonial-era house. On one rainy day during my stay, I sat down and wrote an essay I'd been thinking about for weeks but couldn't find the mental space to draft at home.

More solitude, more creative time exploring my inner life: it was this vision I hoped to look forward to. I hardly remembered what I had wanted half a lifetime ago when I made the massive, permanent choice to bet my life on Brad. I had been so driven by fear and loneliness. Now I feared the future's unknowns, but I knew there could be no worse loneliness than that you find with someone else.

Seeing different places and traveling again was energizing. I jumped at an invitation to speak at a fundraising gala in Austin; I'd never been to Texas, the city sounded fun, and I had a friend there, Hannah, part of a tight-knit group I met online around the turn of the millennium. I won't go into all the different bulletin boards, splinter groups, friendships, and alliances that spun out of those early chat rooms, but I ended up in a small pod that was first a group chat, then a Facebook group, then a Slack with dozens of channels and an all-day, every-day conversation that had lasted for years. They were a rock and an infallible support through the hardest days of Brad's sickness. They sent cases of Jeni's ice cream, cards, flowers, encouragement; I in turn helped organize support when one of them faced grief or hard times. We had celebrated the births of each other's children, gone to one member's wedding, and celebrated divorces together too; Hannah's was the first of these. She, too, had cared for her ex-husband through a terrible extended health crisis, and had found afterward that there was little left of the marriage. I had watched from afar, inspired, as she raised her sons on her own, thrived in a new career, built a joyful life and deep community, fell in love.

I stayed at a nondescript suburban hotel that the nonprofit booked for my talk, but I moved to an Airbnb studio in a trendy part of Austin for the weekend. It felt like a treehouse, wrapped around a spreading oak, flooded with warm November light. The bed was tucked in an alcove, all mine. It evoked the cozy studio I had my senior year of college, a reminder of self-sufficiency every time I sprawled on the solo bed.

Hannah gave me a tour of Austin, including an animatronic Lyndon B. Johnson telling off-color jokes at his namesake presidential library. My one request was to swim in Barton Springs, the spring-fed freshwater public pool I'd read about as a crown jewel of Austin. I knew I wouldn't have time to explore the hill country's many lakes and springs, which spout from the vast Edwards Aquifer in central Texas. Barton Springs was accessible and even had free admission for the winter season. Hannah warned me the water would be cold and said she probably wouldn't swim. At the entrance, alongside displays extolling the Austin blind salamander, a species found only in that spring, I noticed a plaque warning of the springs' "icy waters." I wondered how cold it could be compared to high Sierra streams, but braced myself.

Swimsuit clad, I left the musty bathhouse's chill for warm sunshine and was startled by the pool's familiarity. Sloping lawns, towering oaks, oblong shape, inky water in motion: it looked like an everything's-bigger-in-Texas version of the dammed public freshwater pool in my hometown. Its real name is Sycamore Pool, but many Chicoans just call it One Mile because it's one mile from the town center. Free and open to the public, with shaded lawns and changerooms with lingering childhood scents of Hawaiian Tropic and musty towels, it's the best place to go cool off in a town that routinely sees triple-digit summer days. Both, it turned out, were built as WPA projects in the 1930s. Something about the resemblance to a favorite place from childhood felt symbolic, both comforting and freeing.

The pool was busy for November, with Austinites of all ages and races frolicking. That represents progress: until the 1960s, the pool was segregated, like many public swimming places in the South. A Black teenager, Joan Means Khabele, jumped in as an act of protest and then led swim-ins that led to integration. (Khabele passed away in 2021; a historical marker was added in 2022 and the bathhouse was renamed for her in 2024.) Few of my swims took place in waters with a legal history of segregation, but I'm aware both swimming and access to natural spaces have an inequitable history, whether de facto or de jure.

With so many people swimming, I decided to risk the "icy waters" and jump right in. I was shocked, but for once not by cold. When I bobbed back up, Hannah said Barton Springs maintains a temperature of sixty-eight degrees, year-round. I laughed.

"The Texan who wrote that sign should come to California and try swimming in the Sierra Nevada," I said. "This is nice!"

Hannah raised an eyebrow but let me convince her to get in. We laughed, paddled, snapped selfies, and jumped from the high dive. I looked at my brilliant joyful friend and smiled at how she was thriving. I didn't ask, but she might have agreed with Amy that divorce is our greatest institution. Maybe, I thought, life on my own wouldn't be the shock I feared. Maybe friendships and community could sustain me, recharge me, like the aquifer that filled Barton Springs with water warmer than pessimistic warnings led me to expect. After all, that day, I'd jumped in without so much as dipping a toe, and the water was fine.

~~~

My swim in Austin was my last of the year, and the holiday season that followed was a dark blur. While I was away, Brad's mother worsened, and he flew to Canada the day after my return. She died two weeks later. The girls were devastated. They had not seen her since the day of the pandemic shutdown in March 2020, when their grandparents were visiting from Canada and had to leave in haste lest the border close before they could get back.

I tried my best to support Brad in his grief, but the distance between us was vast. Within a few days, he told me that he had processed it and needed no further support. I loved his mother too, and I mourned her loss, but her death threw us into further limbo. Discernment therapy, meant to produce a mutual decision, had ended in another disagreement. I was increasingly certain I wanted to separate and likely divorce. Brad wouldn't agree to a timeline for moving out, and I wasn't heartless enough to evict a man whose mother had just died, nor to compound my children's grief so soon.

I had also canceled the hysterectomy I was supposed to have the week of Thanksgiving; Brad went to Canada instead. He returned in time for us to visit my family for Thanksgiving. My sister-in-law took a family photo I used on our New Year card that year, one last bit of holiday magic I felt inexplicably compelled to create. The only thing I remember of that Christmas is breaking down on Christmas Eve after our traditional dinner of cracked crab. Crying, I slammed the door and walked a blurry mile in cold rain, as unconscious of where I was going as
~~~

a blind salamander. I ended up leaning on the rough brick of a medical-imaging center across from our old house, the one we brought both our babies home to. The streets deserted, I sobbed out loud, tears and rain mixing on my contorted cheeks.

It was Christmas, our family had suffered a terrible loss, and I was desperate for my husband to move out. The timing could not have been worse. I thought of author and advice columnist Cheryl Strayed and her response to letters from several women who all wanted to leave their relationships but were held back by guilt, anticipatory remorse, reluctance to cause pain, feeling their reasons were inadequate. Strayed described her urge to flee her first marriage: "there was in me an awful thing . . .: a tiny clear voice that would not, no matter what I did, stop saying *go*. . . . Go, because you want to. Because wanting to leave is enough." It was hard for me to accept that wanting to leave was enough. I identify much more with the writer Kimberly Harrington, author of *But You Seemed So Happy*, who wrote on her Substack of "continuously asking for permission to leave from anyone who would grant it, without realizing that's what I was doing. *Someone please tell me it's ok to go even though on paper this doesn't seem technically horrible.*"

I knew I didn't love Brad anymore. I believed we would be happier apart. But part of me wanted an authority figure—a couples counselor; my therapist; Cheryl Strayed; anyone—to give me permission, to say I wasn't a terrible person for wanting to leave a man who almost died.

No authority figure stepped up, but my friend Jill B. did. She had invited me on a hike for her birthday on a sunny January day in 2022. As we climbed windswept kelly-green hills, my conversation turned to the agonized back-and-forth that I was having daily: Should I stay or go? What about the girls? Jill's warm hand on my arm interrupted my mental gymnastics. She looked straight into my eyes, with deep kindness, and said, "Don't wait too long."

CHAPTER SIX

A TALE OF TWO WATERSHEDS

DUNK 21: *Dry Creek, Butte County*
DUNK 22: *(A different) Dry Creek Falls*

I didn't have to wait. A few days after that hike, Brad surprised me.

"My dad wants to come visit in March," he said.

"Okay," I said, hesitating but nodding, dread pooling in my stomach. Houseguests upset the family routine at the best of times. This was the worst of times, and my father-in-law was still grieving the loss of his wife.

"I'm going to move into a new place by then," he continued. "Things are too tense for him to stay here. It would be a disaster, and you'd be miserable. I think it would ruin any chance we might have to save the marriage."

Dumbstruck, I couldn't disagree. How had Brad's stubborn resistance to separating collapsed? My thoughts whirled. It was too soon after his mom's death; it had only been a few weeks. We should wait, for the girls' sake. He was right about his dad staying with us. Did he really think we might get back together after he moved out? How would he find a place so fast? Maybe he could live close by; there were apartments down the street. I should start googling.

Before I could resolve this cacophony of conflicting feelings, instinct took over and I blurted out my first thought. "Don't you think it's too soon, for the girls? Your mom just died a few weeks ago."

"I thought you wanted me to go," he said.

"That's true," I replied. "And you're right it would be hard to have your dad here. But we could get him a place to stay and wait for the girls' sake. You don't have to go so fast." I could hardly believe the words coming out of my own mouth. What was I doing? Brad was conceding what I'd wanted for months, and I was arguing with him?

"We can't put my dad up somewhere else," he said. "He'd be offended not to be hosted and he would know something was up."

Oh, I thought. This shift in his views wasn't about me or our marriage; it was about seeming appropriate to his family, which to my mind had always placed too high a value on appearances.

"Also, there's something I should probably tell you." He looked awkward. "I've been chatting with someone and we're planning to start dating as soon as you and I are separated."

I went from dumbfounded to gobsmacked. He was *what* now? After all his lip service to saving the marriage? After all the couples therapy sessions where he said he was trying his hardest and begged me please not to end it? He was "chatting" with someone? I tried to take a beat but failed.

"Are you fucking serious? Who is she?"

He told me. I knew her, and I'd never liked her. She used to comment with lavish affection on his Facebook posts (platonically, he'd always assured me) and make long and frequent visits in our living room, perfume trailing and jewelry jangling, when Brad was at his sickest and I was at my most burned out. I pulled my lips between my teeth and narrowed my eyes, straining to say nothing. There was a long pause.

"Okay," I said, opening my laptop. "Let's start looking for a place."

~

Winter in northern California starts drab: bare branches, the rumpled blank white sheet of high cloud cover, a sheen of frost some mornings and the thick duvet of impenetrable ground fog on others. The dreary days of January are short, however, and February usually brings a spell of warm weather as well as an explosion of lacy pink and white almond blossoms, a harbinger of real spring and the earliest tree crop to flower. The heady scent of almond pollen, dustier than honey but with its own sweetness, and the steady buzz of rented bees dive-bombing every bloom recurs annually in my memories. Watching orchards in bloom flash by along backroads, the endless rows of trees converging to a vanishing point, always reminded me of home.

My family has an almond orchard a few miles south of Chico, a small acreage my paternal grandfather, George Washington, bought in the late 1960s. He had come to California from Kansas during the Depression to run livestock on a relative's ranch; when he bought the orchard, agriculture in the Sacramento Valley was shifting from sheep and cattle to almonds, walnuts, and rice. The orchard lies at the end of a gravel road on rich silty ground with a small seasonal creek running through it. We called it Cherokee Creek, but it's marked as Dry Creek on the map. The discrepancy stems from its origin near an old ghost town called Cherokee, where a gold mine once boomed, producing millions of dollars. It also yielded surprising diamonds, becoming California's only commercial diamond mine. Though Cherokee once had a population of thousands, it's abandoned today, apart from a never-open local museum, a few crumbling rock walls, and a historical marker commemorating its settlement around 1853 by Cherokee men who came from Oklahoma. In the 1870s, Cherokee had the world's largest hydraulic mining operation, and the area downstream from it, covered with mine tailings and silty soil washed into the valley, came to be called the Cherokee Strip. The soil is ideal for growing almonds. Ever since I read about the mines, I've wondered if someday I might find a diamond, or a bit of gold, winking up at me from the trees or creek bed.

Like most farms the orchard demands endless work. We never lived there when I was growing up; it was too far from town. But my dad took my brother and me a lot, sometimes to run free, sometimes to help a little with seasonal work, though far less was asked of us than of the real farm kids I knew in school. At bloom time, we admired the blossoms and hoped for sunny days and good pollination. In spring, we cracked open downy pale-green baby almonds and ate the tender kernels inside while our dad worked. In summer we picked peaches and plums from the fruit trees planted at the entrance, a sticky endeavor with the itch of peach fuzz, wasps, and the risk of closing your hand around a perfect-looking piece of fruit hiding a juicy cavity of rot or bird damage. Those peaches we tossed aside with a wet thud. At harvest, sometimes we walked the dusty rows of trees to pick rocks and sticks out of mounds of nuts that had been shaken to the ground. A few times I helped my dad move pipe for the old portable irrigation system, before he installed sprinklers and drip. Sometimes we ran down to a disused hog barn, now mostly fallen and full of chicken wire and junk and those ancient pipes, to pick fat spears of asparagus from the vegetable garden. The barn and the asparagus are gone, but there's still a formerly majestic old beast of a green Gran Torino station wagon, the same age as me, rusting away, now with broken windows and target-practice holes.

Before the bloom, there is a dormant season of crimson buds on gnarled bare branches. That's when almond trees must be pruned, a chilly and solitary job my dad has always liked. In pruning season, fallen branches and limbs need to be cleared out of the orchard's rows. One cooped-up day in January 2022, the girls were squirrelly, the sun shone weakly, and my sister-in-law confirmed her kids were also bored. I hatched a last-minute plan to meet them for a little light agricultural labor. The kids climbed trees and rode in the back of the truck over the levee roads. We picnicked on shrimp rolls my sister-in-law brought, ceviche and guacamole I picked up in Live Oak, and hot Cheetos from a stash at the orchard.

When the kids ran down the rutted tire tracks leading to the creek to throw rocks, I started eyeing the water. It was deep in spots and running clear, not muddy. In all the time I'd spent at the orchard, I had never been in Dry Creek beyond a little wading, except when I was taking a filmmaking class in junior high. For our final project, my best friend and I made a short, silent Super 8 movie about seeking treasure and devised a scene in a canoe. We filmed it in February of a flood year, and Dry Creek was raging, muddy and murky.

I had neither towels nor a swimsuit, but I was wearing quick-dry pants and a sweatshirt from a thrift store, so I shooed the kids away, stripped down to underwear, and lay down in the cold water, once, twice, and a third time, on the rough gravel creek bed. Maybe there was a secret mine-runoff diamond lurking in there, but I didn't spot it. It was my first dunk of the new year, and I felt, as ever, strengthened and renewed, like the mythical Greek giant Antaeus, whose mother was the earth and who derived his strength from touching her.

My dad, who has farmed the orchard since the 1970s, has thrown an almond blossom party somewhere around Presidents' Day weekend as an on-again-off-again tradition. Some years it happens; some years weather or obligations intervene. In any case, I try to get to the orchard in February, to walk beneath the fragile drifting snow of falling petals with views of faraway Mount Lassen and the Sierra Nevada. Those views, framed by a wide sky, always ground me, and in recent years I've needed that. February used to be one of my favorite months, a time of hope and promise. Besides flowers, it offered plentiful days off school, the cherry pie my mom always made on Washington's birthday because that was our last name too, and the sweetness of Valentine's candy, even if I never had a Valentine.

My feelings about February got more complicated in 2010, when my mother, aged sixty-four and in the grips of a deep depressive episode, swallowed a lethal handful of medications. My brother and I think she did it on February 21, a Sunday. She had been to church, the last place anyone saw her. Her phone buzzed a busy signal that evening. She never had call-waiting;

she thought it was rude. By Monday morning, though, the phone rang and rang. My brother later reasoned she'd left the cordless handset off the hook so it seemed she was on the phone, and its batteries died.

That Monday was one of those bright false-spring days, marred by underlying worry. Pete thought she just wasn't answering. I wasn't so sure. A few weeks before, she had told her therapist she was planning to end her life. She would hang herself, she told him, and send me an email just before. Later she told me she might not reach out to me. I had just gotten my first smartphone, and I responded to email too fast. She didn't want me to save her. Pete and I made a schedule of wellness checks to call her morning and evening. I wrote the number of the suicide hotline in Sharpie and taped it above her desk. She promised she wouldn't take her life. It was the only promise to me she ever broke.

The day before she died, she came with me and the girls—Nora was four, and Lucy was six months old, chubby and flailing in a BabyBjörn—on a playdate, and then to my house for a lunch of soup and Girl Scout cookies. She seemed happier than I'd seen her in weeks. Now I know she was only more content because she had an escape planned.

I planned on Monday night after dinner to drop by my mom's, allay my concerns, and head to a 7:30 yoga class. I never made it. Her house was dark, newspapers on the porch, and when I peered in a window, I saw her purse slumped on the dining room table. My breath caught and something cramped in my chest. I wasn't seeing the dangling body I feared, but I knew she must be slumped inside too. She wouldn't have left the house without her purse. She had moved there less than a year before, in an impulsive manic episode, and I didn't have a key, so I called 911 and waited, pacing on the lawn, until a kind officer came out to tell me what I already knew: my mother was dead.

I called Brad and asked him to come, but he said he couldn't leave the girls. I was too overwhelmed to insist he call a babysitter, a friend, someone, anyone so I didn't have to be alone. I called Pete, and I don't remember what I said, only that it was the worst phone call I ever had to make. I called my dad. He offered to drive to Sacramento that night, and I was in too much shock to take him up on it. I sat for a couple of hours on the porch in the flashing lights of cop cars, numb with cold and uncertainty. A neighbor I didn't know brought a cup of hot tea and I drank it. I pretended to pray with the police chaplain when he held my hand, and I turned my face away when the gurney with my mother's body clanked over the brick porch.

Only then did I go inside. The coroner said there would be an autopsy and gave me a crookedly photocopied pamphlet, his card, and my mother's purse to take with me. I drove the few miles home and hung the purse on a hook by the front door. That night, I lay in bed, eyes wide open, shivering no matter how many blankets I piled on. I listened to Brad sleep and to the house's deathly hush until Lucy's cries broke the silence and I got up to nurse her.

I have only a few pictures from that spring, and in those I do have, my face is only half in frame. That's how I felt: half there. Brad seemed oblivious to my grief. Soon after the suicide, I started to cry in the kitchen, and he asked what was wrong. He began a demanding new job as chair of his department a few months later, which pushed me further into the role of primary caregiver to the girls. My brother and I were coexecutors of our mom's complicated estate, a stressful monthslong job. Mechanically, I soldiered on. It was only after I dropped everything to care for Brad that I wondered why he had not cared more for me in my grief, or why I had not demanded that care. What I saw as a glaring imbalance in how each of us responded to the other's worst crisis was a key factor in breaking my bond with him.

Every year since 2010, my brother and I had tried to spend some time together around the third week of February, which coincides with the peak almond bloom, a poignant reminder of both family trauma and hope. Now, that cluster of days in February would have a new anniversary. Brad found a long-term Airbnb he could rent for a few months and set his date for moving: February 20, 2022.

~~~

The date was all twos, but the twosome that had long held our family together was splitting into ones. We knew Brad's place was only temporary; I think he chose an Airbnb in part because he hoped he could move back home afterward, whereas I saw it as a waystation before he found a yearlong lease. We were both shocked by the prices of short-term rentals, so he chose one with two bedrooms and two beds total—enough space for him to host his dad but not quite enough to make a comfortable home for the girls. We agreed they would stay with him on Saturday nights. We told them about a week before he moved out, and it was awful. Their story of our split is not mine to tell. I will say only they were angry at me and protective of their father—understandably, since they had nearly lost him.
~~~

Absorbing their reaction was by far the most painful thing about the divorce for me. They didn't want me there on the day he moved out. If they had wanted my comfort or love, I would have stayed home. Maybe I should have anyway. Instead, I planned a day trip with a friend to hike to a waterfall.

I was full of mixed feelings—guilt, relief, sorrow, exhilaration—as I headed out early for the hour-plus drive northeast to the trailhead to Beale Falls, named for a nearby Air Force base. I'd read about the hike in my much-dog-eared swimming hole guidebook, which touted it as "one of those special swimming holes that you can visit all year round." It lies in an exposed, low-elevation area I knew would be hotter than hell on a summer day, so we had picked this hike for early spring instead of waiting for warmer water temperatures.

The hike proved to be an easy 2.5 miles gently sloping uphill along the spring-fed creek to a waterfall, which plummets year-round into a deep, wide hole—a rarity in California, where many waterfalls are seasonal. The falls are also called Dry Creek Falls, after their misnamed creek. (Although it's not far from the Dry Creek at the orchard, they are separate streams, draining separate watersheds.) A few early golden poppies and purple lupine waved in the oak-dotted grasslands, and shiny new leaves of poison oak were unfurling.

The waterfall spouted over colorful striated cliffs into a wide punch bowl–shaped pool below. I balanced on a tumble of rust-colored rocks, eyeing the inky water. It looked cold. Freezing. My friend's dog, who plunges into most bodies of water with abandon, dipped a tentative paw in and beat it back to a rock. I submerged my pool thermometer by the bank. It read forty-nine degrees, but I was sure it would be colder farther out, in deeper waters. But my friend and I stripped off our hiking clothes. It didn't matter that it was February. It didn't matter that even the warmer shallows were the coldest water I'd encountered: colder than Jones Creek, colder than the Pacific. I was going in. I was scared, but I'd been hesitating on the edge of a much colder plunge for months.

My winter-tender legs scraped on rough rocks before going numb. My breath rushed out, and my chest pounded with the shock of the cold. When I stood up, the water draining out of my ponytail felt like pure snowmelt. I was reduced to two competing impulses, to get out and to get back in. I couldn't stay out in the deep water long enough to get an accurate read on the thermometer, but any temperature under fifty degrees made it the coldest of the project. That bone-chilling dunk, and the events of that day, long wished for and long feared, represented a watershed in my life—a sharp break, though a watershed itself is a connected territory, an area of land in which all the water drains to a common outlet. At first, it seems odd that those opposing figurative and literal meanings share a name, just like the two oxymoronic Dry Creeks I visited. But midlife is nothing if not contradictory.

~~~

I had a second motivation in choosing my waterfall destination. The almond blossom party was on, and I realized I could fit in a hike, head across the valley to the orchard, and then go home in a big triangle. It would be a long day, but it would keep me busy enough to distract me. The blossom party is always different. Some years my dad and one of his close friends undertake an
~~~

elaborate cooking project like roasting an entire lamb on a spit, some years it's a bunch of beer and bags of chips on a table. This year fell in between, with grilled bratwurst and hot dogs and potluck salads. There was an extra reason for the celebration, my stepmom Karen's recent retirement from teaching at the high school I'd graduated from years before.

The party was full of the group I mentally called the usual suspects, people who had been my parents' friends when I was a kid and who were like aunts and uncles for me. My family knew that Brad was moving out, and they squeezed me a little longer in welcoming hugs. We didn't talk much about the separation. Most of the family friends didn't know yet, and I wasn't up for party chitchat about it, no matter how long I had known everyone. As an excuse for leaving the party, I took a few walks down orchard rows, snapping pictures of blooms on portrait mode.

Self-conscious about my bare left ring finger, I kept thumbing the callus, feeling for my slender gold band. I doubt anyone noticed its absence. My wedding ring was so tiny, a friend with a fat diamond engagement set once leaned over and pretended to use a magnifying glass to look for it, laughing. I was a little hurt, but she wasn't wrong. I wore my wedding ring on its own, without an engagement ring. Made in the 1920s, it was barely wide enough for its swirling floral pattern, with tiny beading at the edges. Brad and I had found it at a thrift store in 1998, before we got engaged but when we were discussing maybe getting married, at my insistence. We were having a day of sweetness and laughter, and when I wheedled for a ring—not an engagement ring, just a little ring, I said—he gave in. We picked out the pretty band together. It cost $65, an amount we could afford on our grad-school stipends. I think we split it.

I was always fond of that ring. Whenever I took it off, to garden or work out, I hung it on a blown-glass paperweight shaped like a bear, with a long snout that was just right for the ring to dangle on. The paperweight, made by a Chico art glass company, was a long-ago graduation gift from some of the family friends at the party, and I kept it on a built-in desk in my kitchen. I stashed the ring in the same place when Brad moved out and it stayed there for months, but one day I glanced over and the ring was gone. I never found it.

The deep indents on the sides of my ring finger persisted for more than a year, past the time when I lost the ring, and so did my thumb's habit of feeling for it. Old habits die hard, and my marriage lasted nearly a quarter century, a long span of habits to break. No matter how much I wanted out of our patterns, undoing them came as a series of small shocks. It took me months, if not years, not only to stop feeling for my wedding ring but also to wean myself off the codependent relationship I had with Brad. I had wanted out, yet I was hurt—some tiny part of me is still hurt—that he moved on so fast. The spring of 2022 was a series of shocks, kicked off by the big shock of the move-out.

I had known for a long time that separating would be painful. That's why I hesitated for so long to leave a marriage I knew was over in every meaningful sense. Even with that knowledge, it knocked the wind out of me, an instinctual response as reflexive as my breathlessness in the frigid pool below Beale Falls. Later, I told both my brother and a close friend about how startling I had found the knifelike cold. Each of them paused, and each of them said something like, "Well, obviously. It's February, after all."

CHAPTER SEVEN

THE ENCHANTED LAKE

DUNK 25: *Aquatic Park, San Francisco Bay*

DUNK 30: *Golden Quartz Picnic Area, Nevada County, California*

DUNK 39: *Lake Washington, near Seattle*

DUNK 40: *June Lake*

DUNK 41: *Middle Fork, San Joaquin River*

DUNK 42: *Wild Willy's Hot Springs*

DUNK 43: *Tenaya Lake, Yosemite*

Orange scum cracked like the desiccated mud of a low lakebed, the bowl's robin's-egg blue glaze showing in the seams. In a pan, a clump of undissolved cheese powder glued a stray elbow noodle to stainless steel. Both sat by the sink on a summer afternoon in 2022. My jaw tensed. I was not the one who had made boxed macaroni and cheese for lunch.

"Girls!" I yelled into the summer-vacation void of the house. "Girls! Come here!"

They lollygagged downstairs. "What?"

"What's up with these dishes?" I asked.

They stared like I'd asked if water was wet. "We made lunch," said Lucy.

"I can see that. You have to put your dishes in the dishwasher," I said, trying to keep my fast-rising frustration out of my voice. "Or at least in the sink."

"That's not our job," one of them replied.

"Why on earth do you think it's not your job?" I asked. "You made the food and the mess. I need you to pitch in more around the house now that it's just the three of us."

If I hoped this appeal would establish a cheerful new all-for-one attitude toward household chores, I was swiftly disillusioned.

"That's not *our* fault," retorted Lucy. She was about to turn thirteen, and her voice radiated adolescent contempt. "Daddy used to do all our dishes. *You* made him move out, so now they're *your* job."

"Oh no no no," I said, my voice rising to a screech. "That's not how this works." My mind went blank except for pain and rage at how disrespected I felt. I flashed back to a time my mom berated me for leaving the counters and refrigerator door handle sticky after I baked cookies. She had good reason to be angry at my teenage sass and carelessness, but she also used me as a stand-in for her rage at my father after he left her. The circumstances were different, but the emotional parallels were strong. Oh no, I thought again, with my last remaining shred of perspective. My deepest fear had been becoming my mother, and here I was.

I paused to collect myself a little before delivering a lecture about respect and cleaning up after oneself and living in a family, but they weren't listening. Despite what I said, that was indeed how our household worked, and it had been for a long time. For the first few months after Brad's February move, I faced the challenging reality of single parenthood six nights a week. In May, he found a house with a yearlong lease, and we went to a seventy–thirty custody split. In both arrangements, I had long spans with the girls and little time to myself. When they were with him, I missed them and questioned whether I had done irreparable harm with a decision that still felt a little selfish. When they were with me, I was oversensitive to their resentment and anger thanks to my own guilt. Sometimes I walked on eggshells; sometimes I lashed out over perceived disrespect, as with the dishes. We were both wrong: of course they should have rinsed their dishes, but not doing so was normal teenage behavior. They needed my compassion, not anger, which drove us into opposite corners. I understood their pain, but I was also lost in my own.

I would love to say that as soon as I got out of my marriage, I walked a smooth path onward and upward to happy fulfillment. Of course, it wasn't that simple. After an initial burst of exhilaration, I had to work through the lingering resentments, regret over past choices, and anger about the ways the separation and mediation unspooled. As soon as Brad left, however, I knew in my bones that this was no trial separation. It was the real thing. I never missed him, though sometimes I wished for another adult to load the dishwasher or run to the grocery store. Even occasional loneliness came as a relief: at last, I was lonely because I was, in fact, alone.

I might not have missed Brad, but our daughters ached at losing his daily presence. Navigating the tricky waters between selfhood and motherhood had been the hardest part of leaving my marriage. It took me a long time to come to terms with inflicting that pain on them. At the same time, they were my biggest motivation. I did not want them to think that our marriage was what a marriage ought to be, that self-sacrifice and unresolved conflict should be their lot. I did not want them to grow up having never seen a woman choose herself.

My 50 Dunks Project had started giving me more practice making that choice, and I picked up the pace of my swims that spring. I headed out whenever the girls were spending the day with Brad and sometimes when they weren't. With twenty-eight dunks remaining, and about that many weeks until my birthday, I needed a plan to meet my goal. I whipped out a notebook, swimming hole guidebooks, and my calendar and made a big list of dates and destinations. It didn't allow for much spontaneity, but I felt better with a plan. I still hadn't learned to give up control and roll with life, even when chasing joy. I felt like I was leading a double life, on a tightrope between my roles as dutiful single mom and woman waking up to rediscover fun.

Integrating my two selves, the woman and the mother, at first seemed almost impossible, but in April I got a chance. It was the middle of spring break, and Brad and I were splitting the time with the girls. I got the first half of the week, and I rented a beach house for a few nights. Brad then wanted to take them to San Francisco. The easiest thing for him and the girls—though not for me—was to meet him in the city and do a handoff before I drove back to Sacramento. I made the most of it and met a friend at Aquatic Park, a cove near Fisherman's Wharf where she and I used to swim in the Bay, way back in 2000 when I lived in San Francisco. I sold my first-ever freelance article about the open-water swimming club there.

Across the street is a San Francisco institution, the Buena Vista Café; its claim to fame is inventing the Irish coffee. It attracts hordes of tourists, but the diner breakfast is solid, so we met for omelets with sausage patties tucked inside. I wore my swimsuit under my clothes and strolled down to the water after an Irish coffee to bolster me.

I knew the bay was well below sixty degrees, but it felt warmer than the whipping breeze when I left my clothes and keys on the sand and waded out hip deep, alone in the water. At this point, I always faced a choice: sit straight down, dive in headfirst, or fall backward with a big splash to recreate my old favorite, the Nestea plunge. I reserve the Nestea version for warmer waters. Sitting straight down takes the least courage, so that's what I did in the bay. Resurfacing, I heard yelps from a young couple pumping their fists in encouragement. I stood in the wind, feeling the rush of the cold, and dove under, head throbbing with an instant ice cream headache.

As I was gathering up my things, an older woman approached me. "My family said you were crazy," she told me. "I said I was going to go talk to the crazy woman."

"I might be a little crazy," I replied. "I'm turning fifty later this year and I'm doing a project of going to fifty different bodies of water to swim before my birthday."

She responded with enthusiasm, and as we chatted, I saw the young pair who had egged me on stripping down to their underwear. They ran in the water, yelled again, and ran back out. I cheered at them in turn.

"Wow, that was cold!" the woman called out, in an accent I couldn't quite place.

"I know!" I responded.

"We've been here from Israel traveling in America for a year and this is our last week," she explained. "We thought we should do something memorable. We never would have thought of going in if it wasn't for you, but I'm glad we did!"

The fifty dunks were a good way to connect with strangers. People wanted to know what got me in the water, and my explanations seemed to strike a chord. I bet on them resonating later that spring when I dipped my toe in what I expected to be the rough currents of online dating. I made a Tinder profile full of selfies in front of swimming holes, and offered to buy the first drink for matches who could guess one of the locations. It was a good conversation starter. Nevertheless, plenty of guys still went with a boring "hey" and asked few or no questions about me, and then tried to revive faltering chats on Mondays with an apparent burning desire to know how my weekend was. I stopped messaging with such duds quickly. Despite online dating's bad reputation, I found Tinder fun. I picked it in preference to Bumble for two reasons: first, on Bumble the woman messages first, and I was worried that would attract passive men to the app. Second, Brad had told me he was on Bumble and I didn't want to encounter his profile. (Things hadn't worked out with the woman he had been chatting with before he moved out.)

My first post-separation date was with a retired firefighter visiting town. He was warm and flirty on the phone. That continued in person over drinks and dinner; we locked eyes, he reached across the table to touch my hand, and we were off to the races. We ended up in a car makeout session. Making out was not a feature of my marriage, and I'm here to tell you that passionate makeout sessions are even better after decades without them. That date turned into an intermittent, no-commitment fling for the summer and beyond, whenever one of us was in the other's city. Being openly wanted and wanting someone back for the first time in years felt more healing than all the therapy I'd ever done.

I leaned hard into other kinds of fun as well. I went out dancing, tried a ceramics class (cliché though I knew it was), went to concerts. In June, friends and I went to a show high in the Berkeley hills where we watched the sun set over San Francisco as we sang-shouted along to the Indigo Girls' "Closer to Fine," with its poignant lyrics about leaving behind a too-intellectual life, and Brandi Carlile's "The Eye." Both artists were in heavy rotation on the Spotify playlists I made to cope with my jumble of feelings. I blasted music in the car and in the kitchen constantly, favoring breakup songs: the exuberant rage of Alanis Morissette's "You Oughta Know," the energetic girl power of Kelly Clarkson's "Since U Been Gone," the rueful bitterness of "Walking on a Wire" by Richard and Linda Thompson, who were divorcing when they recorded it.

The morning after the Brandi Carlile show, I wasn't sure I could rally for a planned swim day. Excuses rang in my head: it was unseasonably cool, I had driven so much the day before, gas prices were bonkers, maybe I should do chores, such as packing up yet more of Brad's abandoned stuff. But then I thought of the two previous cooped-up summers of smoke and red sun, and I hit the road. My destination, with the alluring name Golden Quartz, lay over rutted, sketchy roads, with zero cell service. I had visions of being stranded, but my Subaru bounced along fine. Nobody else was at the picnic area. I hauled a camp chair to the water's edge and unpacked my book but soon forgot reading as I alternated between dipping in the vibrant clear jade and gazing at it. My reverie continued until the sun began to slant low and a carload of partyers rolled up with dogs and beers, speakers and floaties, and I retreated for home.

Looking back, I wonder why I had started to feel like only my hidden self could have fun, while my mother-self had to be all grim obligation. After Brad got sick, I'd had to be both the responsible parent and the fun parent. I was overstretched as his caregiver, but I also knew it was the girls' one shot at a childhood, and I didn't want it all lost to the sorrow of illness. I drove the girls to counseling sessions and an art-therapy support group and filled out forms and kept their lives running, but I also sometimes chose fun with them over more time by a hospital bedside. During the spring break after his stem cell transplant, we went to San Diego, frolicking on the beach while my in-laws took over hospital duties. When Brad, still blind at the time, had to go to New York for a lifesaving clinical trial during the entire month of December 2016, I stayed home with the girls—often watching movies in my bathrobe while they were at school—because I didn't think they could handle having both parents away. Brad's parents helped him navigate his treatment and the Upper East Side, while I took the girls to *The Nutcracker*, to Christmas celebrations at my dad's house, and to play in the snow.

In this new calamity, I longed to recapture that feeling of the three of us against the world, and I planned a few water-heavy summer getaways with the girls. I was most excited and nervous about an early August road trip to the Eastern Sierra, a dramatic high-desert region south of Lake Tahoe. I wanted to take a week, but the trip was shoehorned into a summer that was already jam-packed, in part because Brad and I hadn't disentangled our lives.

~

Before we separated, we had planned a family trip to Canada for Brad's mother's memorial. Her final wish had been for a summer celebration of life at their cottage in western Quebec, which everyone in the family called The Lake. We had gone there most summers since the girls were babies. Its soft, silky water was like nothing in California, a temperate layer floating above ancient, ominous glacial depths. The trip would be my last swim there and a bittersweet farewell to Brad's family. I was, to put it mildly, ambivalent. The cottage couldn't accommodate the whole extended family, so I had booked a nearby house for the four of us. Now we would have to room together and attend an event at which I imagined I'd be the family villain.

I'd joked to a friend that maybe I could fake a mild case of COVID to get out of it, but in the end I didn't have to fake it. Two weeks before the memorial, exhaustion and a pounding headache led me to a rare nap and an 8 p.m. bedtime. A hacking cough awoke me at 3 a.m., burning with fever. My test line turned bloodred in seconds. In a stupor, I gathered pillows, masks, water, ibuprofen, and dragged myself to the basement to isolate. It was my first bout with the illness, and it felled me. I assumed I would test negative by the time of the memorial, but the days wore on with stubborn maroon positives. With equal parts relief and sorrow, I rearranged and then canceled travel plans. Brad and the girls went without me. My sister-in-law FaceTimed me during the memorial. An hour later, I tested again: finally, it was negative.

The girls and Brad stayed in Canada for a week after, giving me my most extended taste of post-separation, no-kids freedom.

I got an overnight visit from my firefighter fling, but then I ended up traveling for a memorial after all. My aunt, who had many health challenges and lived with my cousin in Seattle, took her life with an overdose of pain medications. It was a sad reminder of our mom, and my brother and I flew to Seattle for the service. The next morning, I made my way to sky-blue Lake Washington, framed by evergreens. I had planned for my thirty-ninth swim to take place in Quebecois waters I'd known for years; instead, I was buoyed by the unfamiliar yet still surrounded by mourning. I floated until I was starting to cut it close for making my flight home, thinking about my aunt, my mother, my mother-in-law, how they all mothered and sacrificed themselves in different ways, how life and loss catch us all unawares.

~~~

Our Eastern Sierra road trip felt cursed from the start. It was a summer of airline meltdowns, and the girls returned from Canada two days late; during their layover, Air Canada canceled not only their Vancouver–Sacramento flight but the entire route. The travel snafu pushed back our start date. The original plan was a night in a hotel, two nights camping near high-desert lakes, and a final hotel night in Bishop, before driving home through Yosemite. I canceled the first hotel and went straight to camping in the high-desert sage and rock tumbles of the leeward east side. (The girls kept saying it seemed like Nevada, a reminder of our ill-fated Elko sojourn.)

Though we hadn't done any family camping to speak of, I'd gone on several mom-and-daughters all-female camping trips
~~~

organized by the same friend who had called divorce "our greatest institution." Amy, mom of two girls, was a seasoned backpacker and outdoorswoman. When the girls were in elementary school, she started an Adventure Club for her daughters and friends, including Nora. The eight girls camped, backpacked, rock climbed, hiked, rafted, rowed, and more. I longed for an Adventure Club of my own. This road trip seemed like a good way to reconnect with the outdoors as a trio.

The east side is known for hot springs, and en route to camping, the girls complained when I took a detour to Travertine Hot Springs, where multiple fissures drip hot water from improbably Seussian rock formations into shallow pools. (The site was once a quarry for the richly veined orange and white marble that adorns San Francisco's ornate city hall.) Our trip already felt like a standoff between what they wanted and what I wanted. They weren't used to me putting my own desires first, and they sat in the car while I followed a short trail through the barren hills. I skipped submerging in those springs, though: the dramatic setting was gorgeous, but the sulfurous pools were the same ninety-seven-degree temperature as the air.

As we climbed to the higher elevation of our campsite, the temperature dropped, clouds gathered, and a chilly thunderstorm struck. I tried to get the tent set up and the rain fly on before it got serious, but the rain became a deluge and the girls wouldn't help. I left the tarp in mud and bundled the wet tent back in the car before it got soaked. To wait out the storm, we made our way to the beachfront of nearby June Lake, deserted except for a couple of kids fishing. I was uninterested in getting wetter and colder that afternoon but hoped to return for a swim the next day.

The rain kept going. And going. And going. Finally it eased. I got the tent upright in the mud, sopped up what I could of the water inside, and busted out a foil emergency blanket as waterproofing for the floor. Then I turned to the problem of food. The rain picked back up; the girls sat in the car while I huddled over the camp stove, heating a frozen bag of Trader Joe's gnocchi and spicy chicken sausage into a delicious mess that we gobbled up in the car. I cast envious glances at our campsite neighbors' RV. As I mused on whether getting soaked while making dinner counted as a dunk and whether we should abandon my hard-won camp setup for a motel, the clouds cracked to reveal a gorgeous sunset.

Rain resumed in the night and puddles gathered in the tent. In the morning, it was clear again, but the forecast boded ill, calling for thunderstorms that afternoon and night. It was a drought year and we were in the high desert, but I'd failed to reckon with the volatile weather of the east side, which is subject to freak summer showers. Our gear was sopping, our sole adult (me) was already tired, and I called it: we would find a room. As we drove away, I stopped at June Lake for that swim. I was already so damp from breaking camp that getting wetter didn't matter much. We weren't the only people trying to wring summer out of an unpromising forecast, and I had to wade far out past the crowds in the cloudy celadon water, like pottery glaze, to get hip deep.

I Pricelined a condo in Mammoth Lakes but wanted to see the sights before check-in time, and before it started to rain again. I hoped to take a short hike to Rainbow Falls, a robust 101-foot waterfall on the Middle Fork of the San Joaquin River. The girls disagreed: the one who had been in Adventure Club wanted to hike. Lucy wanted nothing to do with it. I adjudicated: we would go for adventure.

A shuttle from Mammoth's ski lodge to the hike's trailhead crossed the Pacific Crest Trail, back to the familiar mountain terrain of the west side. Clouds were gathering, and Lucy was worried as we made the short, gentle hike. Every so often we'd hear a distant rumble or feel a drop, but we pressed on to the waterfall, which they both admitted was worth seeing. On the way, I'd spotted a little side trail to a good dunking spot well above the falls, and I insisted on taking a dip, even though the clouds looked darker and the temperature was dropping. The girls urged me to hurry.

As we headed back up the trail, lightning started. We counted the seconds until thunder boomed. Soon, rain came in drenching sheets. Wet already, I gave Lucy my waterproof jacket. I thought of the line between adventure and ordeal. We were crossing into the latter territory, though I didn't want to admit it. Cramps twisted my abdomen and I shook with cold, but I faked fortitude and cheer. During the long wait for the lumbering shuttle back to Mammoth, I looked down at my soaked quick-dry shorts and spotted a rivulet of blood amid the streams of water. The spotting of the previous summer had come back with unpredictable vengeance after the separation. I wondered if too much exertion hiking had made it worse.

~

On the third day, I dialed down the ambition. There would be no hikes, just easy stops. On the way from Mammoth south to Bishop, we found a nature trail that followed a roaring creek through willows, the lush green contrasting with the barren escarpment behind, and the girls chased each other, giggling like little kids. I was surprised to learn the whole east side used to be that green, until Los Angeles diverted its surface water—the story loosely told in the movie *Chinatown*. Kendra Atleework's *Miracle Country*, a memoir of growing up there, describes it, citing the Indigenous name for the region: "Payahuunadu, this country of flowing water, was not named by the Paiutes as metaphor but as literal description of the land before it was visited by outside forces. The valley was desert only when judged by rainfall: scarce precipitation yet so much water, water that used to be snow, flooding out of the mountains, softening the rain shadow."

It was still cool and misty, and I had my heart set on a hot springs soak. The region overflows with pools, most of them undeveloped, and I'd been disappointed by the heat and muck at Travertine. After the creek, we headed to one of the best-known spots, Wild Willy's. The name sounded like a cheesy souvenir shop. But the bumpy dirt road led to a port-a-potty, a wooden boardwalk down to the pools, and little else besides sagebrush and wide views. I warned the girls to expect a clothing-optional crowd, and as I'd expected, they chose to stay in the parking lot. I told them I wouldn't stay too long, compromising my own wishes. I also compromised when it came to wriggling into my suit behind the port-a-potty. I'd have preferred to soak naked, but I worried the girls would be mortified if they came to find me, a sign of my persistent instinct to put myself last.

At the springs, a deep upper pool was the naked spot, whereas shallow, muddy lower pools housed families and shyer adults. I soaked in the chalky white mud and eavesdropped on a group about my age trying to decide which night of their stay to do mushrooms and whether to consume them as pasta sauce or tea. When I got out, the mud clung to my legs. The deeper clothing-optional pool looked good for rinsing, but I was self-conscious.

"Hey, excuse me," I said quietly to one of the nude girls. "Is there room for one more? Sorry, I hope it's okay that I'm wearing a swimsuit."

"Sure! We accept everyone," she said.

"Thanks," I replied. "I'd kind of rather not be wearing it, but my teenagers are in the parking lot."

"It's cool you don't mind if we are," said a guy with a thick beard. "And you're a cool mom to bring your daughters here."

"Thanks," I said. I needed to hear that after the trip's minor disasters. "But of course I don't mind. I mean, clothing optional is the deal here." While I wasn't going to force the girls to go to a naked hot springs, it was worth teaching them to respect the practices of places you travel. I lay back as the group discussed their plans for Burning Man. I could have stayed for hours, but I knew my kids were waiting.

As I got out, I heard an aggressive, shrill voice, addressed to my new acquaintances: "Do you *mind*? We have *children* with us! At least put on a towel when you're out of the water!"

Now I understood why the girl in the pool thanked me. The yelling lady kept berating them until finally, in exasperation, one of the unclothed soakers shot back: "You know, kids have bodies too!"

I had worried the girls would be impatient, but they were chatting and smiling and asked if I'd had a nice soak. I was starting to realize my mother-self and my self-self could coexist.

We spent our last night in Bishop, a small high-desert town that won our hearts with enchiladas, a funky open-air Friday market, and a killer sunset over the mountains. Crammed in a hotel room, none of us slept well, and I awoke knowing the scenic route home through Yosemite would be a long drive. My spotting of two days before had turned into a hemorrhagic period. I'd started taking hormones again to rein in such bleeding, and it wasn't until months later that I realized I'd become much more volatile when I started the hormones. That morning, the girls were supposed to pack while I went to fetch coffee and breakfast. I returned to find the hotel room a mess, the girls in pajamas.

"That took soooo long," they moaned.

"You're welcome. You guys didn't pack at all?" They groaned again. "Nora, do you have my AirPods?"

"They're on the chair," she gestured.

"No, I looked there. Can you look?"

"I put them on the chair," she said, turning to her breakfast. "You must have taken them."

"No, I haven't seen them since last night when you borrowed them from me," I said. "Can you actually *look*?"

She ignored me and I felt a hot flush behind my eyes. "Look," I said, knowing it was a petty thing but already yelling. "*You* borrowed them. *You* didn't give them back. Find them. I'm going to start loading the car." I grabbed my packed bags and stormed out of the hotel room. When I stormed back, they'd made little progress, and I dumped Nora's purse out; there were the AirPods she'd sworn I must have. I snapped. Lucy retreated to the small balcony, crying because of my yelling. That should have stopped me, but when I was in a rage, it didn't. Instead, the only thought in my head was: You think this counts as yelling? You should have heard Cathy Washington in her day.

That morning, however, I was every bit as bad as Cathy Washington in her day, and when my corrosive temper cooled, shame rose. All of us were still upset as we left to drive through some of the most spectacular country in the world. At Mono Lake, I adopted a tone of false cheer to talk up the eerie tufa formations; I was answered with sullen shrugs. I had vague thoughts of going in the water, based on tourist materials that touted its salinity and said swimmers found it hard to sink. I saw an optimistic French family trooping down to the lake's edge in chic striped swim togs, but the quickest of glances at the slimy, buggy lakeshore dissuaded me. (Later, a friend whose husband is high up in California water policy told me nobody should even think about going in that toxic lake.)

We pressed on toward Yosemite, already hungry and road weary. The scenery over Tioga Pass was jaw-dropping, the silence in the car rock-hard, and there was nowhere to stop for lunch. I was starting to despair when we rounded a corner to a view of perhaps the most beautiful body of water I had ever seen. Tenaya Lake is the largest in Yosemite, the sapphire blue of Princess Diana's engagement ring, surrounded by dramatic glacier-carved cliffs. It even had a golden beach and convenient parking.

"I want to be in that right now," I said, turning to park.

We just want to get home, they said. They were hungry. Where were we going to stop for lunch?

"Here!" I said, sounding more chipper than I felt. From what I could tell on the map, there was not a single market, much less a restaurant, until we were well out of Yosemite, hours ahead.

We had a warming ice chest with the last scraps of camping food—some sliced meat, bread, cheese, trail mix, various chips and crackers and apples. That would make enough lunch to get by. It was the best I could do. It was less than a quarter-mile flat walk down to the lake shore. I ignored their groans, changed into a swimsuit in a smelly pit toilet, and marched us down to the lake. I laid out the food on the sole empty picnic table.

"Help yourself," I said. "I'm going swimming."

The water temperature was an ideal seventy-two degrees. I swam far out, away from complaints and the babble of other tourists, the frustrations of the trip dissolving.

"This lake is magic," I said when I got out. "It washes away irritation."

They glared. They were far too old to believe in anything being magic, but I could see a glimmer of temptation in their eyes, a hint that they might overlook their annoyance despite reluctance to admit that any part of this day could be fun.

First Nora waded up to her ankles, then Lucy. And then they both swam, in their clothes. They laughed and smiled and splashed each other and me. I, quiet, let the lake enchant them. We stayed in longer than any of us meant to.

That was far from the end of the day. We still had more than three long hours on the road to Sacramento. But the oppressive, smoldering tension had lifted. The trip had been more ordeal than adventure, but I learned that the mother-self who had to get everyone home and the self-self who wanted to swim and play could converge. If I pursued what I loved, if I got in the lake, my daughters might follow, and we could all be better off. It also taught me I didn't need to work so hard with a grand gesture of a road trip. Our bond was carved from hard rock, deep as a glacial lake; it would survive.

Close to home, I gave into the temptation to mom-splain, as I often do. "I know we were only out there for one night," I said, "but it was great that we could do it on our own! Just women, out in the woods! I know it sounds cheesy, but it's empowering."

Nora laughed. "To me camping is an all-female activity," she said. "I don't think I can remember ever going camping with a man."

CHAPTER EIGHT

ROCKS AND A HARD PLACE

DUNK 45: *A small tributary of the Feather River*
DUNK 46: *Big Chico Creek, near Butte Meadows*

I can do this, I thought, clinging to a rope guide anchored to sheer granite sloping at a dizzying forty-five-degree angle. I looked down to the bare three-inch foothold under my hiking sandal and the sharp drop to more rocks and a silver thread of creek far below, and I hoped like hell that whoever had sunk the pitons into the rock knew what they were doing. The rope was strong, and the stakes hadn't budged when Pete, Evalani, and their two kids, then eleven and five, edged across the dwindling trail. I shuffled behind, alternating between watching each careful footstep and sneaking tantalizing half glimpses at the shaded swimming hole ahead.

I'd wanted to get to this place for years. Every year, I read about it in one guidebook or blog post or another, all extolling its magical seclusion, its clear water, its sparkling granite slides into rushing currents, its double waterfall. Every year, it seemed, I was thwarted. It lay close to California's Highway 70, in the deep and scenic Feather River Canyon, more than two hours' drive from Sacramento. The turnoff to reach the trailhead, via several steep, dusty hairpin turns, was just upcanyon from the starting points of both the Dixie Fire and the Camp Fire. Both wildfires and frequent rockslides seemed to close the highway more than it was open.

This spot was my holy grail, my white whale, and a far greater challenge to reach than I realized until I saw that trail across the granite face. As it turned out, that slippery trail was the easy part of the day. That was partly my own fault. For this day trip, not only had I chosen a tough spot two hours from home instead of an easygoing river day, but I also planned to add hours on the road by looping around to Chico on a further quest.

That mid-August Sunday felt like a last chance in the waning summer. With less than two months left until my fiftieth birthday, it was the forty-fifth dip of my challenge. August has always been a busy month in our family, packed with the last hurrahs of summer travel, Lucy's birthday, and the start of fall sports and school. This year was no exception. A couple of days after we returned, bedraggled, from the Eastern Sierra, the girls turned back around to the mountains for a week of summer camp at Camp Kesem, a volunteer-run, nonprofit, cost-free camp for kids affected by a parent's cancer. They had attended Kesem since 2016, and it was an important ritual and respite for them. They would return home from camp the next day, and after that there were no open days on the calendar before the start of school and Labor Day weekend, for which we would go to Jonesville. Navigating the school year ahead, my first full year as a single parent and a major transition for all, looked like it might be as dizzying as reaching the swimming hole.

~~~

Hunting for swimming holes like the one I sought that day sometimes harked back to a different childhood love of mine. Seeking out secret waters felt like the treasure hunts moms set up as activities at birthday parties, or a magical quest from one of the books I devoured. Sometimes I half hoped that the back of my very humdrum closet would part to reveal Narnia, or that I would solve a real-life treasure hunt like the one in a picture book that transfixed me. Called *Masquerade*, the book featured rich, detailed illustrations of a hare and a lost treasure. It was a treasure quest on a grand scale, with hidden instructions that led to a golden prize somewhere in the United Kingdom. My fascination persisted even though I'd never been to the UK and had no chance of solving the puzzle. Part of me wishes I could write the swimming hole edition: hide a fabulous treasure at each of the destinations I describe, offer a prize and puzzles to get there, lure readers to scour this book for clues, and find their way to places I think they would love.

When I've told local friends I was writing this book, some have begged me not to reveal secret spots, and I've assured them this isn't a guidebook with detailed directions. Of course, people who know the region could find almost any of the places I name; they're all online. I swam in only a few places that felt truly private. The creek deliberately not named in this chapter was one of them.

There's a robust debate in the swimming hole community, if you can call it that, about the ethics of divulging favorite spots. Plenty of secret destinations have been ruined, invaded by hordes of eager Instagrammers and YouTubers and TikTokers.
~~~

Or so locals and old-timers grumble. Many of the places I seek out are remote enough to dissuade crowds, but almost all have had their cover blown. Indeed, that's how I found them in the first place. I've long relied on Timothy Joyce's fat, indispensable *Swimming Holes of California* and Pancho Doll's quirky *Day Trips with a Splash: Swimming Holes of California*, which has hand-drawn maps and marks its entries with icons, including a hand-drawn butt to indicate clothing optional. Joyce has also published a "pro tour" book of harder-to-access swimming holes. Recently, I've also found new-to-me treasures in *Places We Swim California*, by married couple Caroline Clements and Dillon Seitchik-Reardon, which boasts gorgeous photographs. Despite all the information out there, though, there are still secret swimming holes. I've spent a lot of rabbit-hole evenings following link after link to videos the YouTube algorithm serves up or obscure abandoned blogs by adventurers more obsessed than I. My bookmarks folder of swimming holes has dozens of links, some now dead, many with coy but helpful narratives of visiting nameless places. Those write-ups have led me to pore over Google Earth and satellite view and the occasional reverse-image search, checking landmarks and looking for wide spots in a river. The pools those quests have revealed are treasure enough for me, and the *Masquerade*-like search for something hidden in plain sight feeds my childlike love of learning a secret.

All those finds go on my running, ever-lengthening list of places I'd like to swim. When I set the goal of fifty dunks, it seemed like it might be hard to find enough places, but in the end I was overwhelmed by the number I was dying to check out. It's always a pleasure to cross off a long-standing entry on the list, so that forty-fifth expedition had an extra spark. I was even more excited when I realized that it was the same as an unnamed place called "THE Spot" in a rhapsodic blog post by a young Chico State student who chronicled her outings nearby.

When I found that entry, I sent the post to my brother, an avid fisherman who went on countless mountain adventures in the Feather River watershed with his best friend. I thought Pete might recognize THE Spot, and a couple of days later he'd solved the puzzle. He and his buddy had been there, probably two decades before, but he didn't remember exactly how to get there. No worries, I said; he'd confirmed that THE Spot was in my guidebooks, with ample directions. We hatched our plan and met up with a picnic. Pete, who'd last been there as a twentysomething, had forgotten it wasn't easy access. I didn't realize the extent to which those write-ups and my brother had downplayed the difficulty until I was clinging to a rope.

It was easily one hundred degrees in the shade where we parked. We loaded up with backpacks and a picnic cooler they had brought, took swigs of water, and started trudging up the steep abandoned road to the trail. The canyon walls showed evidence of recent fires, but it wasn't as bad as I'd feared. As my brother pointed out, the best features of the area—granite and water—are not flammable. At the trailhead, I couldn't believe how far above the creek we were, given that the guidebook said it was only a quarter mile to the swimming hole. But the creek drops so fast that we quickly came almost level with the creek—the key word being "almost." Soon we could see little potholes, accessible with minor rock hopping but not the main hole. That's when the trail dwindled to that faint track.

Pete and Evalani shuffled their bags around so that she was carrying the food and my brother was carrying their son over what seemed like the most treacherous stretch of trail. My niece skipped ahead, thanks to experience with rock climbing and the impressive footing of a mountain goat. We had to inch around tenacious trees growing out of crevices, and the trail kept narrowing to a small ledge with a view of the next stage: a series of ropes for lowering to a sketchy-looking ladder another anonymous someone had leaned up against a sheer drop. Even that ladder didn't lead directly to the swimming hole; there would be more scrambling after that. But from the ledge, we could see the hole looked as idyllic as advertised.

I was eyeing the ladder with terror when my sister-in-law spoke up.

"We're absolutely not taking our son down that ladder," she said, to my relief.

"I want to check it out," Pete said. "If you want to take the kids back to the little holes downstream, I'll go see if I can find another way to the main hole." He handed their squirmy son to her. Evalani now had a heavy picnic bag and a heavier kid hanging off her. I wanted to offer to take the bag, but I had a backpack of my own.

"I'll go back with you," I said, a little too fast. "Let's leave the picnic bag and make Pete come back for it." He had forged ahead, unburdened. While we were reshuffling, we let by another group of hikers, three young women who looked to be in their early twenties. That seemed like the ideal age range for attempting the ladder route. At twice that age, I had visions of a helicopter rescue out of a deep canyon. I'm committed to adventure as I age; as author Caroline Paul wrote in *Tough Broad*, her paean to older women enjoying the outdoors, "Aging does not have to be a dispiriting spiral. If we shift our mindset, our later years can be a time of exploration, adventure, and joy." Paul talks to women who scuba dive daily, BASE jump, and participate in other extreme sports. Although her subjects are adrenaline junkies, she is clear that people benefit from even modest adventures, like mine. As Paul writes, "You're on an adventure when you're reaching for a goal you've set, feeling physically and mentally engaged, maybe learning something new. It's when you're pushing your comfort zone, and experiencing exhilaration. And having fun. Always fun."

I was determined to wring what fun I could out of this adventure, but retracing our steps was harder than going in; the angle meant I couldn't lead with my dominant foot. My heart banged against my ribs as I watched Evalani traverse it, scree underfoot, with a five-year-old in one arm and that sturdy rope in the other hand. It was the most suspenseful thing I've ever seen in real life. My nephew could have let go or squirmed at any moment and pulled them both down, but my sister-in-law's sure-footed calm and whoever sank the pitons in the granite saw them through.

My brother circled back to us in the little pool, reappearing on the opposite bank. He reported that if we crossed the creek, there was a way up and around with yet more guide ropes along a series of angled granite banks that acted as giant slides into the creek. I chewed my squashed turkey sandwich and poured smashed potato-chip crumbs into my mouth while contemplating whether I was up for the challenge. It would be a shame to come so close and not at least attempt it. I started a spiderlike crawl up the polished stone incline, slipping and scraping my knees every so often. My reward was a long snaking hole of deep forest-green water with a sparkling sandbar, more granite ledges, and a two-tiered waterfall at the back, shaded by trees, with plenty of space to lounge and jump and swim. The girls who had passed us on the trail were there, taking selfies. They said they would never take the ladder down again. I swam up to the waterfall, dove under to touch the rough sand at the bottom, and turned a few somersaults in the brisk water.

I was glad I'd made it to the lower hole but also glad to skip the upper pools above the waterfall, which guidebooks say requires that you squeeze through a crevice in the rocks. *Day Trips with a Splash* reports bluntly: "Here's a swimming hole that discriminates against fat people. To reach it you'll have to scramble between a couple of closely spaced, cabin-sized boulders." One blog post by a tall, rangy water lover described it as a tight fit and said he tore off his swim trunks when they caught on the rocks. If a lanky young guy could get caught, there was no way I'd fit through, even if I could hoist myself high enough.

I wasn't quite done with adventure for the day, though. En route back to our picnic site, I used the guide ropes to slide down the granite chutes into the turbid lower pools. They were as slick as any snaking waterslide and even more fun, since the reward—a cool splash, a rush of bubbles closing over my head—was fresh water without the bleach taint of chlorine. I waded downstream, stumbling over boulders, to rejoin Pete and family, and we packed up our scraps of snacks and trudged downcanyon to our sweltering cars.

~~~

The Feather River Canyon expedition was my second day trip of the week. Before the girls left for summer camp, we'd crammed
~~~

in a quick run up to Chico to meet a litter of six-week-old puppies that my stepmom Karen was raising. We had always been a cat family, mainly because Brad disliked dogs, but I grew up in a dog family. My childhood dog was an ill-tempered beagle mix named Sunny. He loved my dad and me, liked my brother and my mom, and his attitude toward everyone else ranged from toleration (friends) to aggression (the postal carrier). My dad has since then always had a dog, usually male, usually not neutered thanks to my dad's curmudgeonly insistence—half joke, half serious—that it would break their spirit. His dogs were thus prone to running off to seek females in heat. His current springer spaniel is the nicest dog he's ever had, but true to nature had fathered a litter of puppies while my dad and stepmom were taking care of her son's dog, a young purebred Australian cattle dog. Both my dad and my stepbrother disavowed responsibility for the puppies; now Karen was looking for homes for them, and I was considering making us a dog family after all.

I had had fleeting wishes for a dog many times, but Brad had always vetoed it. Conventional wisdom says not to make big decisions in the year following a major loss, and the grief of divorce is such a loss, but I craved change. As a lone woman on the trail, I thought a dog trotting beside me or guarding a campsite might be safer than venturing alone. I also craved unconditional love. Deep down, after my sterile marriage, I wanted to be adored, and a loyal dog would do it as my nest emptied. I also thought it might benefit the girls to have the positive new focus of a puppy and eventual dog companion. I worried about how Lucy would fare after her big sister left for college, and I'd read that teens are statistically happier with a pet to love. I showed them pictures and videos, and they oohed and aahed and said how cute the puppy was. I convinced myself—and them—that would be enough.

Distracted by videos of wriggling, porcine black and white pups, I was too quick to brush off their concerns about how a puppy would fit into our lives, particularly the life of our cat, an unfriendly gray tabby we call Kitty. Her real name is Amaryllis, the name she had at the shelter, and we should have changed it when we adopted her. Amaryllis was too much name for a cat, and we defaulted to the most generic possible nickname. Kitty had been attached to Brad, whose lap she gravitated to since he spent quite a bit of time at home resting. But he couldn't take Kitty with him when he moved out. Cat litter could carry disease; we'd had to get special medical permission to adopt a cat on the condition that he would not clean the litterbox. His new landlord also prohibited pets, so I was stuck with Kitty. The reasons seemed solid enough at the time. I did get angry months later, when Brad adopted a stray cat from his girlfriend's backyard; he had petitioned his doctors and landlord for permission and secured it with no problem. He was willing to change for a sweet, novel cat but not the often-prickly but loyal cat who'd stood by him for years? I asked then if he would take Kitty too; he declined.

Even if he'd wanted her, the girls didn't want the cat to move to their dad's house. They'd had enough change. They protested even small alterations in decor or Brad taking his things, such as the collection of hockey jerseys he'd hung in the basement. I recognized this as their way of exerting control over a situation they hadn't chosen and didn't like, but I was frustrated. Brad got a fresh start and a new living space—and soon a new partner and cat—whereas I was sifting through literal trash he'd left behind and getting scratched by a cat who loved him but not me. Our house held memories at every turn, as well as the detritus of a decade of raising children together, and by staying there I'd saddled myself with processing it all. I was tempted to sell and move, but the girls loved their home and I wasn't about to displace them, as I was once displaced. After my parents' divorce, my mom stayed in my childhood home until I graduated from high school; a day later, moving trucks came and she left town for a new house in suburban Sacramento.

I understood that my kids couldn't take another big life change like moving, but I discounted how big a shift a puppy would represent. The day before the girls left for summer camp, we drove to Chico to meet the litter. The girls squealed with delight as the tiny pups rushed toward us—"roly-poly, pell-mell, tumble-bumble" as the picture book *The Poky Little Puppy* describes it—and cuddled the female we were considering, a runt with a captivating dot on her head. Both girls agreed. She was adorable. They wanted her home with us when they got back from summer camp. We spent the drive home chatting about a potential name. I suggested Dottie. Nora countered with Joni, for two cultural figures she and I both loved: Canadian singer Joni Mitchell and onetime Sacramentan Joan Didion, who had graduated from Nora's high school long before. Lucy said we should spell it Joanie, and it was decided. The puppy had little in common with ethereal Mitchell or steely Didion, but the name suited her anyway.

The girls' timeline worked well with my stepmom's understandable desire to get the puppies out of her yard. Once I said yes, fear seized me: was I going to raise a puppy? I hadn't had a dog since childhood. I had trips planned in September, so I would need to find puppy sitters; I'd have to train her; a dog was a big commitment. But I had committed, so I pointed my car toward Chico.

~~~

My lats and quads already felt sore from pulling myself over rocks as I drove, air-conditioning set to blast. With my kids away and a quixotic mission, I felt as free as I used to in my first car, a mustard-colored, dented 1978 Toyota Corolla. That car, loaded with camping gear, had put-putted up the Feather River Canyon as the first leg of a cross-country drive when I was in college, and it had taken me up and down Highway 99 countless times on blazing days where I rolled the windows down and let my hair blow into irreparable tangles.

These days my car had a lot more power and I wasn't sitting in a sweaty puddle, but the mood was the same and so was my road trip snack (Cheetos). I was still vibrating with the adrenaline of conquering the swimming hole. I cranked up a new-to-me song, Jenny Lewis's "Puppy and a Truck," which starts with the narrator saying her forties were kicking her ass. Her joyful response is to get the titular puppy and bop around in her truck. I wasn't planning on trading in my Subaru Forester, but Joanie could ride shotgun just as easily in that as in any pickup.

My stepmom gave me a travel-size crate for my back seat, and I secured it in the middle so I could see Joanie as I drove home. Nestled in a soft blanket, she snoozed sweetly for the whole drive. I'd watched about a dozen YouTube videos about how to get a puppy settled in, and I followed them to the
~~~

letter, setting Joanie up in a small crate next to my bed. The cat showed no interest in her, nor she in the cat. The puppy was angelic that first night: I got her up twice to pee and heard not a peep out of her otherwise.

I woke up sore but still basking in the glow of the day before. Between puppy tending, I got the house ready to welcome the girls home. The refrigerator was stocked and I'd baked their favorite almond butter–banana snacking cake. Then Brad's car pulled up.

"Hi girls!" I shouted, holding up the puppy. "Joanie's here!"

The girls burst pell-mell, tumble-bumble through the back door, suitcases bumping, pillows shedding dirt, killer scowls on their faces. The return to camp had been more fraught and emotional than any of us had expected; plus, they were exhausted.

Nora glared at me. "Why is there a fucking dog in this house?" she snarled. Either she had forgotten about the puppy, or in her highly emotional state, she couldn't process Joanie's presence, or a little of both. Either way, her angry reaction sent a jab of frustration and regret through me. My smile faded and I drew a thick breath through flared nostrils, pausing to quell my irritation. Our rejiggered family was still a work in progress, but I was learning not to snap back at every teenage inconsistency.

~~~

The rest of August raced by, and I still had five more dunks on my list to hit fifty when Labor Day weekend rolled around. A heat wave was looming, with Sacramento temperatures climbing to an all-time high of 116 degrees. It would still be hot,
~~~

but bearable, in the mountains, so I loaded up the car with the puppy and her crate, sleeping bags, and suitcases, and we headed for the cabin, as we'd done every year since 2010. It was a seasonal ritual that had survived every family and climate calamity, and this year I had anticipatory nostalgia. Our first Labor Day there had marked the start of kindergarten for Nora; this would be her senior year. As her childhood drew to a close, I wanted to feel like we'd wrung every drop out of all her childhood summers.

I'd worried that the chore of packing and planning would be harder for me on my own, but it was easier. The girls pitched in, and I wasn't resentful in advance. They were also a little more tolerant of Joanie, who was at peak puppy cuteness. She had been easy to housebreak, and she slept through the night in her crate. During the day, I couldn't let her roam free in the meadow, but she trotted around a fenced area with the other Washington dogs—two of them, after all, were her parents. The girls and I relaxed into the familiar routine of the cabin. Nora curled up with a book on one of the outdoor beds, and I often spotted her fast asleep, book rolled out of her hand, in the feathery shade beneath conifers.

On our last day, I cajoled her into forgoing her afternoon nap in favor of an expedition. I needed a new place for dunking purposes, and so I scanned the topo maps tacked up in the cabin. There are a lot of alpine lakes nearby, but those are a full-day affair, close as the crow flies but time-consuming to reach over dirt logging roads and faint hiking tracks. Maybe it was the heat, maybe it was the fact of it being our last day, maybe it was the difficulty of rallying a sleepy teen, but I wasn't feeling ambitious enough for a grueling adventure.

I went looking for water in the upper reaches of Big Chico Creek, which runs through Chico and forms the backbone of its enormous, semiwild city park. The creek rises northwest of Jonesville, and its streams flow together at the site of a big Boy Scout camp no more than fifteen minutes from the cabin. The topo map showed a large pear-shaped pond, almost a lake, in the middle of camp, dammed for recreation. I hoped to find the camp empty, so I could sneak in for a swim. The camp was deserted but gated, and extended trespassing looked difficult, so we kept driving. Around a bend, a stand of leafy apple-green willows made a bright splash in the muted grays and olives of the forest. Willows mean water, so I pulled over. A surprising hand-painted sign nailed to a tree read "No Hunting Muskrats." I'm not sure muskrats even live in the area, but there was no caution against trespassing.

Below lay a turbid black pool, fed by a long culvert that flowed into a tangle of Queen Anne's lace and weeds, fringed by the brushy willows and with a steep slope lined by loose rocks. The pool wasn't quite swimmable, but the water came up nearly to my shoulders at the deepest spot. It felt magical, like a hidden fairy pool.

Nora watched me from the bank, ever cautious. "I'd probably feel better if I went in," she said, doubt plain in her voice.

"It's very refreshing," I said, still standing hip deep. I didn't want to push her. Cold water was my thing, but it's not for everyone.

She stood considering. "I want to," she said. "It just looks so cold." She extended a hand as I pulled myself up onto the muddy bank. "I'm gonna do it," she said. "After all, I've never seen you come out of the water without a smile on your face."

Her words gave me a shiver unrelated to the bracing water. My seventeen-year-old daughter might have known me better than I knew myself. She certainly knew herself far better than I knew myself at seventeen, or even at thirty. Her boundaries were solid, her sense of self secure. On that day I started to see the glimmerings of our adult relationship. It was partly that we were sharing the love of water and the outdoors, but even more it was that she saw me not just as Mom but as a full person. After the tension and anger of recent months, that felt as magical as a spring, a headwaters from which our life as mother and daughter could flow. I watched her pick her way down the treacherous wobbly rocks of the bank, and I thought of my recent rock scrambles at THE Spot. This outing was a lot more modest; it might not even rise to the level of an adventure. Even though it lacked thrills, however, this dip brought the same solace and immersion in the moment as any time in nature and water.

Nora's elbows squeezed her goosebumped waist as she eased into the chill. Then she was under, coming up spluttering and laughing, flipping her long hair in a rainbow of flying drops. We both went in again, and we both came out with smiles.

CHAPTER NINE

THE SALT SEA

DUNK 47: *Mediterranean Sea, Cassis*
DUNK 48: *Gorges du Verdon, Provence*
DUNK 49: *Rive Gard, Nîmes*

The high-speed train from Paris to Aix-en-Provence rocketed through the saturated greens of north and central France before depositing me in a familiar landscape of golden hills, blue skies, dusty deep olives and evergreens, the occasional verdant splash of vineyard or silver thread of drought-dwindled river: the same color palette as California, half a world away. I was in France primarily for professional reasons: I gave a talk on caregiving at a massive oncology conference in Paris where I understood almost nothing, even though the proceedings were in English. I was surprised by the invitation, which included business class travel plus four nights in the conference hotel. I'd never said yes to a speaking gig so fast. I added the side trip to the South as a bonus. I'd read about Provence's swimming spots—not just in the Mediterranean but rivers, dramatic gorges, and lakes. I had four swims to go, and I planned to do three of them in the three days remaining of this trip.

"Madame, vous comprenez que cette voiture a une transmission manuelle?" The rental-car agent at the Aix-en-Provence train station pursed his lips as he asked whether I was aware I had rented a car with a manual transmission, his skepticism obvious. Clearly, he had dealt before with Americans who didn't know how to drive a stick shift. But I did, and I had reserved the tiny six-speed Fiat on purpose. My first car, the 1978 Toyota Corolla that I bought for $600 and drove for six years, was a four-speed stick shift. I'd even driven a stick through five years of parallel parking in hilly San Francisco before finally getting my first automatic car in 2011.

"Oui, monsieur, je comprends," I said, nodding and smiling. *"Et je peux la conduire."* Both my French and my gear shifting were rusty, but muscle memory kicked in fast. I'd learned both in the summer of 1988, when my parents were mid-divorce and I was bundled off to France on a language exchange program in which I lived with a family in Brittany, my first big solo adventure.

Now, in September 2022, I was on my first international trip post-separation. I liked the symmetry of returning to France, where I felt comfortable enough navigating both the landscape and the language on my own. As a teenager, I'd worried over conjugations and grammar before I spoke. That feeling persisted during my marriage. Brad grew up with bilingual education in Canada, and his French was far better than mine, so he did most of the talking in French-speaking environments. Now, I plunged ahead, unafraid to make mistakes, and things worked out as long as I smiled and gesticulated and followed a friend's advice to call out a cheery *"Bonjour madame!"* whenever I entered a shop.

It was such a pleasure to be alone, to answer to and compromise with nobody in a place where I knew nobody and I didn't care what anyone might think of what I chose to do. The feeling of being unreachable and unfindable also reminded me of my teenage years. Back then, an ocean away from home, I was self-conscious, a little scared, and homesick to be so untethered from my family, maybe in part because it had shattered. Now, leaving family behind even for a brief week felt like freedom. It also felt like nostalgia for the teenage days when I could drive that stick shift car away from my house and not a soul knew where I was. Not to sound too ancient and Kids Today about it, but I worry that my daughters' generation has no inkling of that kind of freedom. They and their friends all share their locations with each other on their phones, to my bafflement. They're equally baffled when I tell them being untraceable brought me strange joy, even though I didn't do all that much with the privilege. I used to drive back roads lined with almond orchards outside of town late on warm summer nights when the farmers had the sprinklers on, windows down, to catch the cool air, scented with damp dirt and the faintest whiff of marzipan.

Then, I found that expansive selfhood close to home; now, I had to travel far afield for it. In the rental-car garage at the Aix station, I found my tiny cream-colored Fiat, stepped on the clutch to start it up, and plugged in my phone. I had hours of blazing-hot afternoon ahead of me, no obligations, a full tank of gas, and working GPS. It was time to find some water.

~

I'd been to Paris several times before, so I didn't feel much compulsion to pack in sightseeing while there. I wanted to take the trip as it came, leaving myself open to serendipity and surprises and curbing my perfectionism, in both travel and life. When married I had planned every trip and most of our lives. I overfunctioned, letting Brad retreat into passivity, and as a consequence I was like a poster child for the gendered division of cognitive labor. My gendered overplanning was supplemented by a family culture of aspirational doggedness. If my dad took us on an expedition to cut down a Christmas tree, he was sure that the best one always lay over the next ridge or in deeper snow. I had long applied that reasoning to restaurants, logistical arrangements, airline routes, hikes, and yes, swimming spots. Now, I was trying to teach myself that sometimes good enough was more than good enough.

I was staying in an unfamiliar neighborhood, the untouristy fourteenth arrondissement, and I did no research on the restaurants. Years as a restaurant critic had made me impatient with the foodie culture of bagging trophy restaurants and nitpicking about food. It was France; the food was going to be good, and if it wasn't, there would be another meal later, and more every day after that. On my first night, I stumbled into a pocket-sized restaurant serving lacy Breton crepes, earthy with buckwheat. They reminded me of my time in Brittany as a teenager. Over the bar was a chalkboard for the specials, on which someone had written, in curly French handwriting, *"Liberté, Egalité, Beurre Salé!"* ("Liberty, Equality, Salted Butter!")—a play on the motto of the French Revolution, which touts fraternity instead of dairy products. That's a manifesto I can get behind, I thought, as I relished both the savory, salty crepe and the liberty of my sidewalk table. I know people who don't enjoy dining alone, but I long have—if for no other reason than people-watching and eavesdropping. When I was married, our date nights invariably consisted of obligatory dinners out, which felt less than festive for two reasons: they overlapped too much with my work as a restaurant critic, even when I wasn't working, and our stilted conversation left me lonely. Sitting alone with a book and my observations, though, rarely did.

Solo restaurant dining could hit a little different, however, when it was by necessity rather than by choice. I thought of M. F. K. Fisher's essay on dining alone, the first entry in her *Alphabet for Gourmets*, in which she laments that as a single woman known as a food writer she was rarely invited to friends' homes to eat: "I have often eaten an egg and drunk a glass of jug wine, surrounded deliberately with the trappings of busyness, in a hollow Hollywood flat . . . and not been able to stifle my longing to be anywhere but there, in the company of any of a dozen predatory or ambitious or even kind people who had not invited me. That was the trouble: nobody did." Instead, they mumbled a variant on "we wouldn't dare cook for you," a refrain even I, an infinitely lesser food writer than Fisher, had heard from friends who feared I might be rude enough to turn my critic's palate and words on the food they cooked. I always said I'm not working when I'm dining with friends, but they still demurred. Fisher's initial plan for combating this loneliness was a sign of her times, when a woman dining alone might still be scandalous. "I resolved to establish myself as a well-behaved female at one or two good restaurants, where I could dine alone at a pleasant table with adequate attentions rather than be pushed into a corner and given a raw or overweary waiter." Her project succeeds; at her favorite restaurants, "they knew I tipped well, they knew I wanted simple but excellent menus, and above all, they knew that I could order and drink all by myself, an aperitif and a small bottle of wine or a mug of ale, without turning into a maudlin, potential pick-up for the Gentlemen at the Bar."[3]

Times have evolved a little since Fisher's 1940s, though not as much as one might hope. When I became the restaurant critic for the *Sacramento Bee* in 2017, I received a reader letter marveling at the idea of a female dining critic and asking if I would feel comfortable dining alone: "Dining out is a couples thing and it seems strange that the girl pulls out her own credit card." (I didn't always pull out my credit card; I often had Brad pay, but that was to maintain my anonymity, since our last names were different.) On my last night in Paris, being a woman dining alone served me well. I had gone to see the stained glass of Ste.-Chapelle, as Notre Dame was still closed for repairs, and was making my way back across the city through the chichi sixth arrondissement. I aimed toward a small, no-reservations bistro a food-writer friend had messaged me to recommend, with a minuscule, standing-room-only oyster bar attached. That sounded casual and easy, possibly a good choice for my last night, but when I got there, I felt shy. The bar was packed, and I couldn't figure out how to elbow my way in without feeling like a nuisance. The streets and cafés nearby were likewise packed, with smoking laughing crowds spilling out in the waning September light.

After a few anxious laps around the fountain at the center of the square, I attempted the restaurant—not Michelin starred, but recognized by the guide and with a reasonably famous chef—instead. It looked full, but it was first come, first served, so I took a chance, approaching the sharp-faced woman at the host stand with my best *"Bonjour madame!"* and my politest request in French if they might possibly have a table for one, even though I could see they were very busy. Her face broke into a smile. Yes, madame, it would be her pleasure, they had one last table—a tiny one in the middle of the dining room, commanding a view of the whole restaurant and the lively, beautiful street. I didn't pull out my phone to take pictures, so I've forgotten some of what I ordered, but I recall superlative pig's trotters, of all things: pork, gelatinous with connective tissue and cooked to melting tenderness, shredded and formed into a precise baton and crisped to a deep brown. For dessert, I had *îles flottantes*, diaphanous clouds of meringue on a sea of delicate custard.

When I finally abandoned my table, I walked into the night satisfied but eager for more adventure, fully embodied, fully in the world of pleasure. For a long time, France and the French language were semi-intellectual pursuits for me. I wanted to know things, to learn the language, the history, and the art. On this trip, I wanted to feel things: food in my mouth, water on my skin. I had thought that I might fire up the dating apps in search of a fling here or there, but once on the ground, I was not in the mood to break my reverie with a man. That waited for me back in San Francisco; the firefighter had pledged to pick me up from the airport and host me for a night. This time in France was only to please myself, and what pleased me was independence, food, and swimming.

~

Solo travel meant that there was nobody to be annoyed when my obstinacy reared up and I insisted on long detours or a meandering search for the perfect swim. Leaving Aix, I headed for a nearby blob of blue on the GPS, the closest water. It turned out to be a shallow puddle of a lake with only one or two other beachgoers, shores lined with flyblown algae and deserted snack stands at the edge of a sparse, depressed-looking sprawl of a town. I knew I could do better: the Mediterranean. I aimed for Cassis, east of Marseille, which I'd read had a lovely beach. First, though, I had to get through Marseille. At some point my GPS gave up the ghost, and I navigated the city by following signs for *les plages*.

It reminded me of the first chapter of my French I textbook in high school: our first verb was *aller* (to go), and the locations people went, in the lesson, included *la plage* (the beach), *la piscine* (the pool), and other recreational spots. Marseille has a reputation for being more workaday than picturesque, but the azure of the sea by the city was glorious. Every spot I pulled over, though, seemed not quite right: some had no parking, some were rock piles, one was actually a boules court, and another had closed changing rooms and a loitering crowd in the parking lot that made me nervous about leaving my luggage in the car. I'd been driving for more than an hour and still hadn't swum anywhere, and my hotel was another hour back in Aix. Getting to Cassis from the middle of Marseille would take forty-five minutes or more, but what else did I have to do?

The route snaked up to breathtaking views over seaside limestone cliffs that form steep inlets called the Calanques, then plummeted into Cassis, a town of butter-yellow buildings and slick tiled streets leading straight to the sea. To the right was a harbor full of sailboats and yachts; to the left, crowded pebbly sands overlooked by a dramatic steep bluff. Here there was a semipublic bathroom for changing into the swimsuit I fished out of my suitcase. I regretted not bringing a towel, and with no companion it was a little worrying to leave my things unattended on the busy beach, but I arranged my bag, topped with sunglasses, next to someone who looked trustworthy enough. I waded out and in one moment the sea felt like home. I thought of what the Romans called it: *Mare Nostrum*, our sea. Now it felt a little bit mine as I bobbed around in the cool surf, soothing compared to the open ocean but still strong enough to pull me back and forth. The saline water buoyed me. The Mediterranean is one of the saltiest seas in the world, thanks to evaporation. It was once far drier and saltier. More than five million years ago, the present-day Strait of Gibraltar closed, cutting the Mediterranean off from the Atlantic. The sea dried up almost entirely until the Strait of Gibraltar opened and the sea refilled in a massive gush called the Zanclean Flood. The flow is thought to have been hundreds of times more powerful than the discharge of the Amazon River. It was hard to imagine such geological extremes at this gorgeous, gentle Mediterranean beach, but the setting itself was evidence of recovery from even catastrophic drought.

Before leaving the beach, I took some selfies in the amber light bouncing off the cliffs, sunglasses on, hair wet, a gold pendant dangling in my cleavage. I thought they might make a good update for my dating-app profile when I got home. Then I got an ice cream cone—the flavor, *tarte au citron*, was the same pale yellow as the light and the town's stucco walls—and headed inland to my hotel, a small one on the outskirts of Aix. It was 7 p.m., and I was a few minutes away, when my phone rang with a French number. It was the hotel's desk clerk, asking if I knew when I would be arriving. *Désolée*, I said. I lost track of time *à la plage*.

~~~

On my second day in the South, I planned a day trip eastward to the Gorges du Verdon, a dramatic canyon where in typical years people kayak upriver between the steep walls. This was not a typical year: the water was low, but there was a large reservoir at the mouth of the gorge. I wouldn't have time for a long adventure hiking the canyon walls anyway. The gorge lay what looked like an hour and a half to the east, through agricultural backroads, not the charming market towns that made Provence famous. I spent the morning poking around the open-air market of Aix: boxes of dusky plums and web-skinned, green-striped melons and crenellated split tomatoes; fragrant open bins of peppercorns and cinnamon sticks and crystalline spice-flecked *sel fou* (crazy salt); and tourist-bait dish towels next to fine jacquard linens. I was looking for traditional espadrilles, rope-soled fabric shoes that were trendy when I was in high school, for a friend, and found them in a shop called Cendrillon, French for Cinderella. At a busy restaurant next to the town square's big fountain, I lingered over *pissaladière* (flatbread with anchovies) and espresso with a tiny chocolate biscuit.

Finally, I set off. I wound through gnarled almond orchards, clearly much older than my dad's, some crisp and gray with drought, and passed lavender fields and olive groves, but few houses or towns. This was a more remote, wilder part of southern France than the postcard version of Provence or the Côte d'Azur, and it reminded me again of home. When I reached the gorge, there were a few inns and campgrounds and snack shacks, but little evidence of many visitors, and no wonder. The
~~~

canyon's forbidding rock faces descended to a trickle of river far below the bridge, and slick stretches of pallid clay bordered the milky turquoise waters of the diminished river—named Verdon for its green hue—emerging into the reservoir it fed, Lac Ste.-Croix.

The morning's brilliant sunshine had given way to overcast skies that gave the landscape an eerie hush and washed its faded colors out still more, and there were few people at the lakeside. I wasn't sure whether I'd parked in a permissible lot or on someone's private property; the whole area seemed borderline hostile to visitors. It was a long trek down loose shale to the low water, and I had to change behind a tree, but once I braved some mud to launch myself into the cool water, the lakebed fell away quickly. The calm of back floating, with the canyon walls towering above, washed away the stiffness of the long drive.

I took another route back to my hotel, climbing up to a medieval hillside fortress town and making other stops when I spotted a rare farm stand or a little beekeeper's store selling honey and lavender. Lost in the landscape, I failed to notice the dropping gas gauge, and I was far from any sizable town. The little Fiat got good mileage, but it wouldn't hold out forever, so with spotty cell service I trawled Google Maps for gas stations. As the low-fuel light glowed orange, I approached the outskirts of a charmless town choked with rush hour traffic. When I pulled into a station, I realized I hadn't reckoned with the array of different fuels in Europe. This one was hydrogen only and closed up tight. Now I was getting anxious. The next closest station was three miles off my route, in traffic, but I was too nervous to press forward, so I turned north, sweating as the gauge edged a little lower. This station had actual gas, as well as other fuels I didn't recognize. My shoulders lowered two inches, and I blew my breath out as I pulled up alongside a pump, on which the octanes of petroleum were all higher than in the US, starting at ninety-three rather than our eighty-seven. Which should I use? The car required a specific type. Luckily, a sticker on the fuel door specified: ninety-five only.

That's when I noticed that the pump—and every one of its neighbors—bore a red ribbon, lettered with the words *"HORS SERVICE."* Out of service. Great. Was there another station nearby? Was there fuel to be had anywhere in the South of France? Google had failed me; I was going to have to ask. I marched into the convenience store, where a woman eyed me from behind the counter without a hint of friendliness. *"Bonjour Madame!"* I singsonged with false cheer. Her faintly hostile gaze held. *Excusez-moi, madame*, I said. I need ninety-five—and I trailed off. I didn't know the word for octane and wasn't sure I'd gotten the number right. French has a deranged numerical system above sixty, and it's possible I asked not for *quatre-vingt-quinze* (four twenties fifteen) but four-twenties-fifty. Oh well. I waded back in. *"Alors,"* I continued. *"Avez-vous de l'essence?"*

She looked at me as if I were a simpleton. *Bien sur*, she said, in a heavy Provençal accent that was almost as hard for me to understand as it clearly was for her to understand me. But of course we have gasoline, madame. We are, as you see, *une station-service*.

But it is all out of service, I stumbled.

No, madame, they are not, she replied in the tone one uses with a none-too-bright child. Her patience with the idiot American clogging up the line had expired.

The customer behind me, thank goodness, spoke a little English and took pity. I explained my problem, he spoke to her, and he turned back to me. "The pumps are not out of service. You must ignore the signs," he said.

Ah, *naturellement*, I thought. I thanked him and slunk out, embarrassed and relieved and triumphant all at once. My little Fiat's thirst slaked, I drove back to the main highway and high-tailed it to the hotel for a second dip of the day, this time in a pristine tiled pool. After that, I had a reservation for dinner at my hotel's restaurant. The garden restaurant, with fountains and formal arched allées bathed in moonlight, was both peaceful and lively, with other guests traipsing back and forth to the bar and a courteous waiter who humored my French. Solo travel might have its stresses, but the pleasure of independence, self-sufficiency, and both knowing and satisfying my own needs was greater.

~~~

On the next day, my last in France, I had a 5 p.m. train ticket on the TGV back to Paris, with plans to fly out in the morning. My hope and plan was to make it to the Pont du Gard, a two-thousand-year-old arched, tiered Roman bridge and aqueduct near the ancient town of Nîmes. I wanted to swim in the river below. Like the Gorges du Verdon, it was a solid hour-and-a-half drive from Aix. I was tired, and I wasn't sure the river was even swimmable. Besides, the forecast called for rain—indeed, for thunderstorms. Would it be worth it, I wondered. Would I even have time? Could I stand another long day in the car
~~~

followed by a train trip? Should I stay in Aix, go to the Cézanne museum there, and call it a trip?

My doggedness kicked in. It was September 14. I had three weeks until I would turn fifty, and I had racked up forty-eight dunks. I wanted to complete the forty-ninth in France, and I had a particular reason for wanting to visit the Pont du Gard. I had last seen it nearly forty years before, when my grandparents took me on an epic summer trip to France and Italy. We had visited it then while staying in the nearby town of Uzès, where the springs that fed the Roman aqueduct rise. I remembered many swims from that trip: several in the Mediterranean, one at the hotel pool in Uzès where I was shocked by women sunbathing topless, one wonderful one deep in the gorge of the shady Tarn River in central France. There we had stayed in a converted castle, which awed my childhood self. It still serves as a hotel, and I'd hoped to squeeze in a repeat visit on this short trip, but France is too big. A pilgrimage back to any spot I remembered would do.

It sounded cool to swim in the shadow of a feat of engineering two millennia old. The Pont du Gard was built without mortar, its enormous limestone blocks hewn to fit together like puzzle pieces, so well constructed that it withstood floods that collapsed much newer bridges. Clogged by mineral deposits, the aqueduct fell into disuse after a few centuries, but the structure became a toll bridge and allowed vehicle traffic as late as the 1990s, when UNESCO and the French government intervened, cleared the site for pedestrians, built a museum, and created two entrances: one, the Rive Droite (right bank), that leads to the river and swimming, and the Rive Gauche (left bank), the more popular, with direct access to the museum.

I pointed my GPS to the Rive Droite. This day trip led through the heart of picturesque Provence, far more populous and less bleak than the previous day's. I had plenty of gas, but I wasn't worried about finding a station—or people accustomed to American tourists—if I ran low. At the Rive Droite, the deserted parking lot made me worry I was in the wrong place. But a short walk led to changing rooms and a terrace overlooking the bridge, with a restaurant and an ice cream and souvenir shop. The water was deep, wide, clear enough to see the pebbly riverbed, banked by some rock bluffs for jumping, and empty of swimmers. *Parfait.* The colossal aqueduct towered above, its arched symmetry rippling in reflection.

The air was sticky warm, though the predicted thunderstorms had held off. As I waded out waist deep, the water's cool liquid embrace revived me. I paddled and splashed like a kid, torn between staring at the imperial majesty of the bridge and diving under to swim across. I scanned the river surface. I'm no daredevil; the first rule of river swimming is to respect the river and its currents. I didn't know this spot, or whether undertows might lurk beneath the bluffs. Then, I heard guttural shouts, in German or maybe Dutch, and splashes. A gaggle of tall men had appeared on the rocks and were jumping in, then swimming across. I took their cue and did the same, turning somersaults in the deep water at the far bank, floating to gaze up at the engineering marvel of a lost era.

The kid in me wanted to stay in forever. The adult in me had a nagging worry about missing my train and felt I should take a closer look at the historic bridge, since I had come all this way. Both of us wanted lunch. I dripped dry and walked out on the bridge's modern platform. Up close, the enormous stone blocks were even more impressive, but what I loved best was the graffiti, ancient and modern, carved into the stone. There were dates from the eighteenth century, initials and names, and variations on "I was here" in French.

Before I set out on the road back to Aix—which also led to my train and the flight home to California and hectic responsibility—I needed lunch. What's more, I wanted a good lunch, one that would feed the part of myself that had recently been learning to identify not just what I needed but what I wanted, in food and sex and love and all the other parts of life. I thought of M. F. K. Fisher dining alone, and how even as great a writer and independent a woman as she had struggled to know and satisfy her appetites: "It took me several years of such periods of being alone to learn how to care for myself, at least at table," she writes. "I came to believe that since nobody else dared feed me as I wished to be fed, I must do it myself, and with as much aplomb as I could muster."

All my aplomb mustered, I asked for a table with a view at the café. In French, I ordered a big salad with salt-cod fritters and candy-striped Chioggia beet slices and a mustardy vinaigrette that tasted exactly like the one my host family in France had served on all their salads in 1988. My glass of rosé beaded with condensation like pavé diamonds in the muggy heat. When I held it up, the precise rows of graduated arches on the Pont du Gard refracted and shimmered through it.

I thought about the graffiti, from ancient to just old, on the bridge. At one time they were a defacement. Now, it had turned historic, and moving: evidence that people don't change. From a long-dead Roman stonemason to an anonymous traveler of 250 years ago on down to me, we all want to know who we are and that we are here, wherever that might be. We want to show our work, express our desires, mark our time and place and essential selves. I had lost touch with all of that for a time, but here in the shadow of a bridge that has stood for two thousand years, damp from a river running swift and deep despite drought, I felt fully myself. The homesick but awed girl my grandparents brought to this river long ago and the hungry woman she had become were one again. In that moment, regret and age no longer stung as I faced the next chapter of my life. I had made, or at least started, the changes that I needed to make to feel joyful about turning fifty—which, after all, was the tiniest fraction of the age of the stones I stood on. They had held for millennia thanks to clever, careful engineers and craftspeople, who fit together the rocks they had without using mortar or supports. On the smallest of scales, I had been remaking and hewing the materials of my own life, so I too could stand alone.

CHAPTER TEN

THE GOLDEN RIVER

DUNK 50: *South Yuba River*

"Shotgun!" Nora called out, approaching the car after an early dismissal from school.

"I'm already in the front, beeyotch," retorted Lucy.

"Okay, but I'm on aux," Nora said, and plugged in her phone to play DJ. "And I get shotgun on the way back." Her sister gave a gracious nod.

"I'm so glad you guys are coming with me," I said. When I was a teenager, my mom would no more have fibbed to spring me from school than she would have jumped off a rock into a cold river; I was so worried about getting in trouble that I didn't even skip on senior cut day. Now, however, I lied without hesitation to the school secretaries that my kids had doctor's appointments. If I'd learned nothing else in three decades, I'd at least figured out that school left no such legacy as a permanent record for absences to mar.

It was noon on October 6, my fiftieth birthday, and we were headed to my favorite river. From the day I started the 50 Dunks Project, I knew where I would take my fiftieth swim. I saved the best for last. My favorite swimming river, the South Yuba, boasts a string of deep, clear pools sunk in granite-lined canyons, with access points called "crossings," for spots where bridges were built in gold-mining days. The crossings comprise pockets of a state park, not connected to each other, jewel beads strung on the chain of the river. I'd gone to some of its gems earlier in my fifty dunks, but I'd skipped the most accessible, called simply the Highway 49 Crossing. It's situated at an old arched bridge where the river flows under Highway 49—a north–south state highway that runs through the richest regions of California's old goldfields. The road's number, of course, references the Gold Rush's beginning in 1849, but the number also felt a bit like kismet, a happy coincidence that I would swim there on the day I left forty-nine behind.

Thanks to a quick turnoff from the main road with a big parking lot and an easy staircase down to the water, the Highway 49 crossing is always packed on summer weekends. The crowds leave used diapers and beer cans at the water's edge, and whooping teen daredevils do half gainers off the bridge. People flock for good reasons: the rainbow bridge arcs over the deepest turquoise water anyone could hope to see. The silver boulders form swimmable tunnels, jumping and sunbathing platforms, sleek slides, and gentle water chutes to ride down. It's a swimmer's paradise, and everyone in the area knows it.

On that Thursday in early October, I figured the show-offs and beer swillers would be at school or work. But my kids and I were taking the day off, despite the busy whirl of fall activities, work, and puppy training that had sucked me under since I'd returned from France a few weeks before. The girls and I ignored all that for that one day. When I turned forty, I had yearned for a big party. At fifty, I was still midstream in the big transition of finding out who I wanted to be in the next era of my life. Although the relieved giddiness of the early days of separation had faded, I could see the outlines of a new life in which I could choose the forms of care and community that satisfied me. On my big birthday, I just wanted to enjoy myself.

Amid devastating political turmoil and climate disaster, seeking pleasure for personal satisfaction sometimes feels merely hedonistic. I tell myself I'm overdue for a little hedonism, but I think the whole world is. As a society, we have the resources for everyone to enjoy the outdoors or whatever leisure pleasures move us, but those resources are hoarded by megabillionaires and the systems of late capitalism. Whether by economic necessity or by choice or both, so many of us have internalized those American values of always striving and working harder, but it doesn't have to be this way. I don't have a political solution, though as a recovering bossy big sister I do have a lot of ideas of what I would do if I were in charge.

Part of what my 50 Dunks Project did for me, however, was help me realize I don't have to be that bossy girl. I can relax my grip, stop trying to control people and outcomes. When I was Brad's caregiver, I always wanted to have a plan B, C, and D, a contingency for every contingency. When he had recovered enough to care for himself, I tried my hardest to push him into being the partner I wanted. Both approaches failed, and both were signs of my fears and dissatisfaction with myself and my choices. The solution was to choose new things, not to reengineer the choices of the past. That started with choosing myself and what I loved. The release of the body, entering in-the-moment flow states: these were boons water brought me. Our culture relentlessly pressures women, especially, to forsake our joy in service of others, leaving us depleted. I had to learn both what I needed and what I wanted. I had to become embodied again after years of alienation, whether that happened in a quick dip in a spring-fed creek to cool off from a heated fight or a once-in-a-lifetime swim beneath a long-dry Roman aqueduct or a stolen birthday dip at the river I love best with the two people I love best, the ones I made with the body I tried to deny for so long.

The drive from Sacramento to the Highway 49 bridge was long for an afternoon, but that brief moment of normal teenage bickering over the front seat was the only hint of a fight. Sticky Cheetos dust glued my fingertips with salty orange sludge. Candy-sweet Taylor Swift melodies rang out, and I sang along in a few simple harmonies. I failed to stop myself from tearing up when Nora played Swift's "The Best Day," a song about how days the little Taylor spent with her mom were always her favorites. In honor of my birthday, the girls didn't even roll their eyes when tears glistened in mine, and they laughed at all my jokes, even the corny ones.

We rolled up to a near-empty parking lot and left the air-conditioned chill of the car. It was ninety degrees, but it felt cooler. By early October, the post-equinox slant of the sun has softened the blast furnace of midsummer, and heat doesn't beat off the pavement the way it does in July. I remember that feeling from childhood birthdays too. The thermostat often hit the same triple-digit temperatures as in the dog days, but the punishment was over. That meant river season was almost over too—a bittersweet paradox, but all the more reason to seize the day.

The cascade of big rocks and crumbling asphalt steps that led down to the water were in shadow, so they didn't burn to the touch. We picked our way down the stairs to find two or three people on the rocks, one with a little dog hopping from rock to rock. I'd left Joanie, still not fully vaccinated, with a pet sitter, and when I saw other dogs, I was glad.

The gravelly shore crunched under my sandals, and the low water lapped calmly. A muddy scent like freshwater fish mingled with the mineral aura of warm granite. A scraggly tree brushed my skin as I tucked our towels and water bottles under a rock. As usual, I waded in first. The girls followed and yelped, then followed again as I dove under and swam far out before I surfaced. Bubbles tickled my face, and the river pulled my hair into a single stream behind me. I tucked and catapulted myself into a somersault, all the water play of my life converging in a moment. Tumbling under, bubbles streaming out of my nose, I was a mermaid calling out to my mother to watch me, a daughter grinning after my dad tossed me off a high bank, a big sister competing with my little brother to swim the farthest while we held our breath, a mother rating her daughter's handstands, a woman in my element.

The girls caught up and we paddled to the slick granite slides of the far shore, where we hoisted up and basked and slid again and again. I swam upriver by myself for a few minutes, swooping under rocks, and every time I surfaced, I could hear, faintly, my daughters' high silvery laughs as they teased and splashed each other. The river's flow was low so late in the dry season, but still deep and clear enough to see fish twenty feet down. I expected warmer water with the autumn river so slow moving, but the longer nights and temperate days in the high country had already started to take effect.

The little shrieks the girls and I each gave when we submerged were a reminder that the cycle of the year was turning. First would come the rain—if all went well and it wasn't another disastrous drought year—and then the snow, layering the Sierra crest with the water California would need for the dry summer ahead. Then, in spring, the ice, spackled thick as buttercream on a wedding cake, would melt and swell the rivers, making them dangerous. Every year, somewhere in California, less cautious swimmers than I die from jumping into the froth at the base of a waterfall, braving an irresistible current that pins them under an unseen boulder, or simply drowning, open mouthed, from the gasp reflex. Water is always more powerful than we are, and it obeys far simpler rules than those that humans impose on ourselves. It freezes when the temperature drops, melts when it rises, runs downhill when there's a slope or a gully, and creates one when there isn't.

The rules of water do, however, lead it to behave differently in different landscapes and at different times. When rivers are young, they snake around, try to find their course, meander through the landscape, unsure and ungrounded. As they age, they anchor into place, cut deep into canyons, define their course. The rivers I love most are not all that old—they drain a young land, as the writer John McPhee tells us in his brilliant narrative of geology, *Assembling California*—but they have settled into the solid rock of the Sierra Nevada batholith, finding their place in the world. Rivers are always deepening, carving into the landscape, reshaping themselves as they become more what they are meant to be. Their trick is to keep flowing, and to avoid being left behind like an oxbow lake, or polluted beyond repair.

The Yuba was, for a time, all but ruined by exploitation. One of the richest mining regions in California, it produced vast amounts of gold through equally vast amounts of hydraulic mining. As McPhee puts it: "In a year and a half, hydraulic mining washes enough material into the Yuba River to fill the Erie Canal. By 1878 along the Yuba alone, eighteen thousand acres of farmland are covered. Mud, sand, cobble—Yuba tailings and Feather River tailings spew ten miles into the Great Central Valley. Tailings of the American River reach farther than that." I can vouch for him on the latter; to this day, nearly 150 years after hydraulic mining was banned, piles of round cobblestones line the trails along the Lower American River, as far downstream as Sacramento's suburbs. Upriver, McPhee writes, hydraulic hoses with jets "the diameter of a dinner plate" carved whole valleys and canyons that did not exist before the Gold Rush, hundreds of feet deep and a mile wide, "manmade landscape on a Biblical scale." The damage along the Yuba watershed was so extensive that it sparked the country's first environmental regulation. In 1882, a wheat farmer sued the North Bloomfield Mining Company, which operated on the Yuba, and Judge Lorenzo Sawyer ruled against the mining company. North Bloomfield—called Humbug City until hydraulic mining uncovered millions of dollars' worth of gold from what McPhee called its "flushed-away ground"—is only a few miles from my swimming spot.

The land looks different now than it did before European settlement, but it has recovered enough to look wild again. By the end of my forties I felt like I had been hydraulically mined, exploited—unlike a river, with my own consent and by my own choice—for my emotional gold, all the care and support I could provide to others. My inner landscape was little better than a jumble of mine tailings and toxic sludge. I was in danger of drying out entirely, sinking into a mudpuddle before the waters ever reached the Delta, much less the ocean. My drought years may not have been as cataclysmic as hydraulic mining or climate change, but they shifted my world. In danger of losing myself altogether, I turned to water—sweat, tears, rivers flowing to the salt sea—for relief. All that water swept my life into a new channel, one that nourishes me far more than my previous default mode of draining myself for others.

When I chose the ocean for my first dunk, I wasn't thinking of it as the place where all waters lead; it just seemed right to jump in a big body of water to kick off a big goal. It was more meaningful than I knew. I worked my way backward, upriver like a salmon, to the places I was spawned and the places that nurture me in adulthood. Along my way of taking the waters, I took the full cure: I can't recall a dunk that didn't involve sweat, tears, the salt sea, or some combination of them all. The pleasure and catharsis of water was my way of coming back to myself, but anyone whose streams have been diverted, who has stagnated, will find that redemption in their own way.

After a few hours of sliding and swimming and jumping, our fingertips were pruny and rough—pinkled, as Nora used to say in the bath when she was a toddler—and the water was shaded, the sun nearly level with the rim of the canyon. I asked a stranger to take our picture; in it, the three of us lean against each other, dripping, the reflection of boulders and bushes shimmering in the topaz water behind us. Then it was time to head back for a birthday dinner with the three of us and my brother. As I climbed the uneven rocks to the parking lot, my legs had the sweet, heavy, tired feeling that stopped short of exhaustion, the hallmark of an adventure that stopped short of an ordeal. Nora climbed into the front seat, and Lucy plugged in her phone to provide music from the back. I took one last glance back at the evergreens, the steep canyon walls, the graceful bridge, and the platinum rocks holding a rough rhombus of the emerald river in a solitaire setting, like the kind of ring I'll never wear again.

"Thank you for coming with me," I said to my daughters. "I couldn't have asked for a better birthday." Their smiles mirrored my own face back at me, and they slumped into their seats, tired too.

My tangled ponytail dripped Yuba River water down my back, and the air-conditioning raised goosebumps on my tanned forearms as I swung the car around. I waited until I was sure the highway's sharp curves were clear. Then I pointed the car downhill and punched the gas, ready to follow the winding course of the river home.

AFTERWORD

ALL THE DUNKS AND BEYOND

Early in writing this book I realized that if I described each of my 50 swimming and dunking destinations, my readers would drown in the metaphorical waters of all the details. I've chosen instead to focus on those that revealed the most about the story I wanted to tell, rather than writing an exhaustive catalog or guidebook. For extra-curious readers, however, here's the list, with a short comment on each dunk—and after that, an update on my post-fifty life.

1. Dillon Beach, California; April 2, 2021 (see Introduction).
2. Wilbur Hot Springs, California; April 26, 2021. Day trip with a friend to the sulfurous pools of a retreat center in bleak Lake County.
3. Lake Natoma, Folsom, California; May 9, 2021. Paddleboarding in chilly waters on Mother's Day.
4. The Flumes, West Branch of the Feather River, Paradise, California; May 16, 2021. Expedition with an old

friend to hike on the catwalks of flumes damaged by the Camp Fire, plus a river swim among volcanic rock.

5. Jones Creek, Jonesville, California; June 20, 2021 (see chapter 1).
6. Butte Creek at Cherry Hill, Butte Meadows, California; June 20, 2021 (see chapter 1).
7. Putah Creek, near Winters, California; June 29, 2021. A quiet reading date with a friend by the grassy, oak-dotted bank of a fast-flowing creek on the valley's west side.
8. South Fork of the Snake River, Swan Valley, Idaho; July 7, 2021. A quick dip at a fishing ramp, in a slower spot near the shore of the Snake's mighty torrent, while the kids threw rocks in the river, before a stop for huckleberry ice cream.
9. Jenny Lake, Grand Teton National Park, Wyoming; July 8, 2021 (see chapter 2).
10. Teton River, near Driggs, Idaho; July 9, 2021 (see chapter 2).
11. Natural Bridges Cavern on Coyote Creek, Calaveras County, California; July 29, 2021 (see chapter 3).
12. William B. Pond Recreation Area, Lower American River; August 4, 2021 (see chapter 3).
13. Clark's Hole, North Fork American River, near Auburn, California; August 12, 2021 (see chapter 3).
14. Russian River estuary, Goat Rock State Beach, Jenner, California; August 15, 2021 (see chapter 4).
15. A small reservoir in Sonoma County, California; August 15, 2021 (see chapter 4).

16. Edwards Crossing, South Yuba River; August 30, 2021 (see chapter 5).
17. Salmon Hole, Upper Bidwell Park, Chico, California; September 4, 2021. Labor Day hike with an old friend and our daughters to a beloved Chico swimming hole.
18. Monterey Bay; October 15, 2021 (see chapter 5).
19. San Lorenzo River, Henry Cowell State Park, near Felton, California; October 16, 2021 (see chapter 5).
20. Barton Springs, Austin, Texas; November 13, 2021 (see chapter 5).
21. Dry Creek, near Nelson, California; January 17, 2022 (see chapter 6).
22. Dry Creek Falls, Spenceville Wildlife Area; February 20, 2022 (see chapter 6).
23. Thermalito Diversion Pool, near Oroville, California; April 1, 2022. Roadside stop with a quick dip in Lake Oroville after a hike to see wildflowers at the North Table Mountain Ecological Reserve.
24. Harrington Way river access, Lower American River; April 3, 2022. Jumped in after a long walk with a friend.
25. Aquatic Park, San Francisco Bay; April 13, 2022 (see chapter 7).
26. South Fork of the American River, near Lotus, California; May 4, 2022. Day trip to get out of the house while Nora was isolating with COVID, which she caught at junior prom (you know you're Gen Z when . . .); I read a book by the fast-flowing river and watched rafts run the rapids.

27. Garcia Bend Park, Sacramento River; May 30, 2022. A rare, muddy Sacramento River dip, after failed attempts to organize a bigger Memorial Day kayaking and paddleboard outing.
28. Upper Lake Clementine, near Auburn, California; June 8, 2022. Playing hooky from work and paddleboarding with a friend on a small, quiet reservoir on the American.
29. Willow Creek, Butte County, California; June 11, 2022. Yet another tiny creek near Jonesville, this one muddy banked from running through meadows.
30. Golden Quartz Picnic Area, near Washington, California; June 19, 2022 (see chapter 7).
31. Bear Hole, Upper Bidwell Park; June 23, 2022. A swim at a classic Chico State University party spot surrounded by distinctive black basalt, quiet on a sizzling Thursday morning. The next day, I picked up the hometown paper at my brother's house and found that a reporter had been there, too, taking pictures and interviewing swimmers.
32. One Mile, Bidwell Park, Chico, California; June 24, 25, and 26, 2022. In my hometown for a few days, I jumped in the waters of Sycamore Pool (also called One Mile) every day. (For more discussion of this site, see chapter 5.)
33. Thermalito Forebay, Oroville, California; June 24, 2022. Paddleboarding expedition with my stepmom to a human-made body of water on the Lake Oroville reservoir system; I disobeyed posted signs prohibiting swimming off the dock.

34. Butte Creek Trestle, near Durham, California; June 25, 2022. Back in the '90s, when I was away at college, my dad used to take my stepsiblings to this old train trestle to jump off into a deep hole. Years-later FOMO lured me there on a scorching 105-degree day, and thanks to a newly constructed bridge there was no way to get to the creek except by walking over the train trestle, which I did while thinking nervously of the train scene in *Stand By Me*. Bravado overrode my caution while sticky melted tar glued my flip-flops to my feet. The creek was overwarm and choked with nasty algae, but I went in nevertheless.
35. Hanauma Bay, Oahu, Hawaii; July 3, 2022. On a short trip to Hawaii with Lucy and my brother and family, we went to this snorkeling bay (and learned sometimes it closes down for the Obamas to snorkel there).
36. Waimea Falls, Oahu; July 6, 2022. A slightly crowded swim in a botanical garden on the North Shore of Oahu, beneath a waterfall. I overheard someone asking the lifeguards about the water temperature, only to get response like, "Yeah, man, we used to know the temperature, but we've been doing this for a while and, like, the water is pretty nice?" I told them I keep a water thermometer handy because I go to a lot of swimming holes, and that the water was a balmy seventy-five. "You're hired," an attendant said, and for a minute I wished I could quit all my other obligations to sit by a waterfall-fed pool in Hawaii, just for the chance at a solo after-hours swim.

37. Kaneohe Bay sandbar, Oahu; July 7, 2022. Rented kayaks to paddle out to shallow, very warm waters over a sandbar in hopes of seeing sea turtles; picnicked in the boats and got stung by jellyfish.
38. Upper Emerald Pools, near Emigrant Gap, California; July 27, 2022. Two friends and I went on an easy day trip to a glassy, cold waterfall-fed pool surrounded by jumping rocks. It's a spot I've also taken my kids, with fascinating geological formations—striated rock in a range of colors, turned on its side in a way that bespeaks old faults or the smashing together of tectonic plates—and some of the prettiest of them, striped in pink and orange, form a small slot canyon above the main hole just wide enough to explore.
39. Waverly Beach Park, Lake Washington, Kirkland, Washington; July 29, 2022 (see chapter 7).
40. June Lake, Mono County, California; August 4, 2022 (see chapter 7).
41. Middle Fork of the San Joaquin River, above Rainbow Falls, near Mammoth, California; August 4, 2022 (see chapter 7).
42. Wild Willy's Hot Springs; August 5, 2022 (see chapter 7).
43. Tenaya Lake, Yosemite; August 6, 2022 (see chapter 7).
44. Lake Berryessa, near Winters, California; August 12, 2022. A quick jump in a shadeless reservoir on the valley's west side, with a long walk out to the water.
45. A tributary of the Feather River; August 14, 2022 (see chapter 8).

46. Forks of Big Chico Creek, Chico Meadows; September 4, 2022 (see chapter 8).
47. Plage de la Grande Mer, Cassis, France; September 12, 2022 (see chapter 9).
48. Pont du Galetas, Lac de Sainte-Croix, near the Gorges du Verdon, France; September 13, 2022 (see chapter 9).
49. Pont du Gard, near Nîmes, France; September 14, 2022 (see chapter 9).
50. Old Highway 49 Bridge, South Yuba River, near Nevada City, California; October 6, 2022 (see chapter 10).

~~~

Since completing my fifty dips, I haven't stopped swimming and seeking out new bodies of water, from cenotes in Mexico to turquoise coves along the Italian Riviera. I've also kept revisiting familiar haunts and finding new places to love in California. (The first thing I did upon finishing this book was to throw a bag in the car and head to Yosemite for three days of seeking swimming holes with my partner—whom I met because I had a picture of our mutual favorite swimming spot on the South Yuba on my online dating profile.) It's inspired me to do more as well; I finally got that hysterectomy in February 2023. Overcoming my fear of going under the knife freed my body from the storms of hormones and anger as well as bleeding and constant low-level pain I hadn't even realized I was experiencing. As Kristin Scott-Thomas says to Phoebe Waller-Bridge's character in her famous monologue about menopause in *Fleabag*, "It
~~~

is the most wonderful fucking thing in the world. . . . You're free." Recovery, despite my fears, was no big deal.

My path to freedom was not always linear. Nobody flipped a switch on my milestone birthday and released me into the world healed, whole, and happy. But day to day I'm now far, far happier than when I was mired at the bottom of that U-shaped curve in my late forties. Life after fifty has more rewards than I would have thought, largely because learning to choose myself in the water and out of it has helped me live my best life. In the year following my fiftieth birthday, I embarked on intensive therapy that gave me tools to move on from resentment and anger, further improved my relationship with my daughters, and most of all helped heal my relationship with myself. One of the practical suggestions that the therapy offered for interrupting a cycle of anger was to immerse one's face, or one's whole body if possible, in cold water.

It's no accident that I felt most like myself, and best, in the water. Science now shows that cold-water plunges increase dopamine, reduce fatigue, and improve well-being. Physician Mark Harper's *Chill: The Cold Water Swim Cure*—one of many recent books about cold plunges and wild swimming—suggests cold-water swimming as a therapy for a host of ailments and surveys the physiology of its effectiveness, from vasoconstriction in the skin to its engagement of the sympathetic and parasympathetic nervous systems. If you're inspired to read more, there are many less scientific paeans to water, from Jessica Lee's lovely memoir of swimming in icebound Berlin lakes, *Turning*, to Katherine May's soothing, inspiring *Wintering: The Power of Rest and Retreat in Difficult Times*, in which May finds her most electric and helpful reset in wintertime ocean swimming. May says the water "makes [her] feel alive," having "deliberately thrown [her] body into a kind of crisis to force it to find an equilibrium again."

Along the way to finding my own equilibrium, I also did psychedelic-assisted therapy, a deeply meaningful experience that helped rewire some of the negative thinking I absorbed from my earliest days. My midlife crisis wouldn't have been complete without a tattoo (a California quail, our state bird), along with getting that puppy. (Don't worry, I skipped a sports car; I need my Subaru for the dirt roads that lead to the best rivers and lakes.) Joanie has learned to swim and is much calmer now that she's a full-grown dog. The girls are reconciled to her presence, though Kitty still has doubts. Both my daughters come with me on swim days sometimes, though they are busy with a watery obsession of their own; both are competitive rowers. Nora is now away at college, but on road trips to regattas with her friends she sometimes makes them pull over by lakes and rivers, however cold the water. She usually sends me a selfie of her dunks.

Every time someone, whether a stranger or my own child, sees me happy in the water and jumps in after me, it adds to my own joy. If you're feeling, as you read this, that you need something of your own to shake you out of whatever doldrums you happen to be in, I hope you'll find a way to dive in midstream, too, whether literally in water or figuratively into whatever brings you back to yourself. If this book moves you to start your own quest, I'd love to hear about it; I can be reached via my website, kawashington.com.

ACKNOWLEDGMENTS

I owe my first thanks to my late agent Beth Vesel, who was a devoted champion of my first book *Already Toast: Caregiving and Burnout in America* and a tremendous support in the early development of *Midstream*. I also extend my gratitude to her former assistant Lauren Champlin and to Frazier Moore for their graciousness around the practical and legal matters that followed her sad and unexpected passing. Rest in peace, Beth.

My agent Aemilia Phillips is a wonderful, enthusiastic advocate and reader, always warm and supportive. I am grateful to her and the team at Stuart Krichevsky Literary Agency for shepherding me and *Midstream* to publication.

It has been a delight to return for a second time as a Beacon Press author. Thanks to my former editor Catherine Tung for seeing the potential in this project, and to her wonderful colleague Joanna Green for taking it on after Catherine's departure. I'm grateful to Joanna for her kind and keen editing, encouragement, and thoughtful shaping of the manuscript. Having started my career in writing as a copy editor and sometime proofreader myself, I am always relieved to have sharp eyes combing over my words; copyeditor Teddy Turner and proofreader Damian Shand greatly improved this book in countless small ways. Louis Roe designed a cover that made me gasp out loud when I first saw it; it beautifully reflects my book's themes and setting, and I'm grateful for his creative vision. My deep thanks to the entire Beacon team for being unfailingly supportive and hands-on, as they were with *Already Toast*.

Thanks to Writing x Writers for hosting me at an inspiring writing residency in Chamonix, France, in June 2025 and to my fellow writers there for their supportive comments and conversation. Special thanks to residency leader Pam Houston, whom I've admired since my college boyfriend gave me *Cowboys Are My Weakness*, for her answer to my question about how to create patterns in memoir without repeating yourself when, say, you're writing about doing the same thing fifty times. That conversation broke open a dam in my brain at the exact right time to help me finish this book.

Many more writing colleagues and friends were instrumental in the development of this book. Molly Watson talked me down from many a freakout, talked me up with many a pep talk, and generously read the manuscript at a critical moment. Trina Wood and Alice Fong-Yi Liu kept me on track with accountability dates and insightful feedback. Rae Gouirand's online Scribe Lab helped keep my flickering writing flame alive for years, and Rae has long been fiercely supportive and encouraging of my work, including this project. My Chico writing group—Bonnie Pipkin, Sarah Peterson, Dylan Latimer, Molly Paul, Juni Stevens-Banerjee, and Eric Hartmann—helped break me out of a long writing drought and offered enthusiasm and encouragement in response to early drafts. If I still lived in my hometown, as I sometimes wish I did, I'd never have left the group in a million years. Extra thanks to Sarah for lifelong friendship and for coming with me to Bear Hole, Salmon Hole, the Flumes, and many hikes and swims before and after the ones in this book. Lots of thanks and love to my long-ago roommate Jordanna Bailkin for constant loyalty, support, and humor, and to the best group chat: Jana Lithgow, Hannah Meehan, Jill Hermann-Wilmarth, Alexis Brett, Meghan Kelly, Terri Coles, and Lisa Schmeiser.

Chris Cheetham read my entire 50 Dunks Project blog the day after we met, and more recently he listened to me read every single word of this book aloud, more than once, during revisions. After every chapter, he never failed to tell me it would win a prize. I'm lucky and grateful to have the kind of support and love every author needs, and the most fun, most enthusiastic companion for the best river days.

Thanks always to my dad Ernie Washington for pushing me in that creek and for always making sure I knew you were proud of me. To my stepmother Karen Washington, thank you for your constant kindness and support, and for Joanie. To my brother Peter, thanks for finding the way around the ladder, for putting in the hot tub at the cabin, for all those summer days holding our breath underwater and digging islands, and for always being there. Nora and Lucy, it is my life's great joy to watch you become your own women, in the face of all our family has been through; thank you for your love.

To Mom, Grandma, and Grandpa, I wish you were here; thanks for everything that made my life possible.

I am profoundly grateful for the many volunteer organizations that work to keep all my favorite rivers and waterways in California and beyond as wild and scenic as possible, especially the South Yuba River Citizens League, the American River Conservancy, Save the American River, and Friends of Butte Creek. In appreciation, I have donated a portion of the advance for this book to support their work.

Thanks to everyone who told me about their favorite swimming hole or came with me on a river day. You're all invited on the next one, any time.

NOTES

INTRODUCTION: TAKING THE WATERS

Page 5: "Studies have shown . . . that happiness dips": For an extended discussion of this phenomenon, see Jonathan Rauch, *The Happiness Curve: Why Life Gets Better After 50* (New York: St. Martin's Press, 2018).

Page 5: "the average age of the American caregiver": See AARP Public Policy Institute and National Alliance for Caregiving, *Caregiving in the United States: 2025 Report*, July 2025. Available online at aarp.org. In the 2025 report, the average age is given as fifty; in an earlier 2020 report, which I cited in my book *Already Toast: Caregiving and Burnout in America* (Boston: Beacon Press, 2021), the average age was forty-nine.

Page 6: "I recently heard Maggie Smith . . .": Lyz Lenz and Maggie Smith, "'Weird cicadas' with Maggie Smith," in *This American Ex-Wife: The Podcast*, produced by Zachary Oren Smith, Substack, 55:03, December 23, 2023, https://lyz.substack.com/p/weird-cicadas-with-maggie-smith.

Page 7: "There is a seductiveness to water": Bonnie Tsui, *Why We Swim* (New York: Algonquin, 2020), 249.

Page 7: "a cure for everything: salt water": Isak Dinesen, *Seven Gothic Tales* (New York: Vintage Books, 1991; original publication 1934), 39.

CHAPTER ONE: A SPRING-FED STREAM

Page 22: "one of the last naturally spawning populations of spring-run Chinook salmon": See, for instance, Ramona deNies, "Meet Butte Creek: California's Secret Stronghold," Wild Salmon Center (February 2024), https://wildsalmoncenter.org/2024/02/13/meet-butte-creek-californias-secret-stronghold/.

Page 23: "like Laura Ingalls Wilder": See *The Long Winter* from Wilder's Little House on the Prairie series, which I read and reread as a child. *The Long Winter* is a bleak book, the sixth in the series, set in 1880–81, when the Ingalls family had settled in South Dakota; blizzard after blizzard cuts the town off from supplies, and the family nearly starves and freezes. The book made a strong impression on me as a child, and I reread it during the pandemic. Laura Ingalls Wilder, *The Long Winter* (New York: Harper & Brothers, 1940).

CHAPTER TWO: ACROSS THE GREAT DIVIDE

Page 40: "As Jancee Dunn writes . . .": Jancee Dunn, *Hot and Bothered: What No One Tells You About Menopause and How to Feel Like Yourself Again* (New York: G. P. Putnam's Sons, 2023), 5. On the history of medical ignorance of menopause, see Heather Corinna's excellent *What Fresh Hell Is This? Perimenopause, Menopause, Other Indignities, and You* (New York: Hachette, 2021), especially chapters 2 and 5.

Page 40: "Only about 20 percent": Corinna, *What Fresh Hell Is This?*, 91.

Page 41: "There's been a robust cultural dialogue": While there are too many articles, think pieces, and books to cite here, Dunn and Corinna are good starting points, as are Jen Gunter, *The Menopause Manifesto: Own Your Health with Facts and Feminism* (New York: Citadel, 2021), and Susan Dominus, "Women Have Been Misled About Menopause," *New York Times Magazine* (February 1, 2023), https://www.nytimes.com/2023/02/01/magazine/menopause-hot-flashes-hormone-therapy.html.

Page 42: "dismissive of women's pain—as recent studies . . . show": See, for instance, Lanlan Zhang et al., "Gender Biases in Estimation of Others' Pain," *Journal of Pain* 22, no. 9 (September 2021).

For a deep dive into women's pain in an ob-gyn setting, I recommend the podcast *The Retrievals.*

Page 43: "I'd been trying to save the marriage": Maggie Smith, *You Could Make This Place Beautiful: A Memoir* (New York: One Signal Publishers, 2023), 100.

Page 47: "Research shows quantitative gender differences in leisure": Anne Helen Petersen, "Who Gets 'Quality' Leisure?," *Culture Study*, Substack, November 20, 2022, https://annehelen.substack.com/p/who-gets-quality-leisure. Petersen's article links to a number of time-use studies regarding gender differences in leisure time, as well as considering the qualitative gap.

Page 48: "Women make the lion's share of holiday magic": See Olivia Storz, "Holiday 'Magic' Is Also Unpaid Care Work," Institute for Women's Policy Research (December 23, 2021), https://iwpr.org/holiday-magic-is-also-unpaid-care-work/. I've written about this conundrum in tongue-in-cheek fashion but had difficulty practicing what I preached; see Kate Washington, "How to Do the Holidays Like a Man," Grok Nation (November 30, 2017), https://groknation.com/relating/holidays-like-man/.

CHAPTER THREE: TAMED AND SCENIC RIVERS

Page 54: "I also didn't tell him": Mira Kirshenbaum, *Too Good to Leave, Too Bad to Stay: A Step-by-Step Guide to Help You Decide Whether to Stay In or Get Out of Your Relationship* (New York: Plume, 1997).

Page 56: "The best time to move on": Anne Helen Petersen, "Leave Before There Is Nothing Left to Leave: Ask a Divorced Person, Round One," *Culture Study*, Substack, September 7, 2022, https://annehelen.substack.com/p/leave-before-there-is-nothing-left.

Page 58: "working toward a Maidu cultural park": See the Mountain Maidu Summit Consortium website, https://www.maidusummit.org/.

Page 58: "Cal Fire and other fire agencies have begun consulting with Indigenous groups": Pre-colonial Indigenous land and fire management contrasts sharply with the policy of fire suppression adopted by European Americans in the last hundred years, but the pendulum has begun to swing toward acceptance of prescribed burns and land management using so-called good fire. While the literature on this topic is far too vast to cover here, two recent books that look at fire in the West through personal lenses make wonderful starting points: River Selby's *Hotshot: A Life on Fire* (New York: Atlantic Monthly Press, 2025), and Manjula Martin, *The Last Fire Season: A Personal and Pyronatural History* (New York: Pantheon, 2024).

Page 60: "the only federally designated": Ashley Shult Langdon, *Mildly Scenic: A Trail Guide to Sacramento's Lower American River* (Sacramento, CA: Mildly Scenic, 2024), 9.

Page 61: "Sacramento-born Joan Didion": Joan Didion, *Where I Was From* (New York: Knopf, 2003), 20.

Page 66: "From the late 1940s to the early 1960s": See "Swimming Hole in North Fork Opens June 27," *Placer Herald* (June 17, 1949); "Clark's Hole Is Popular with Swimmers," *Auburn Journal* (August 11, 1949); and similar articles, accessed on newspapers.com.

CHAPTER FOUR: A RESERVOIR WITH A VIEW

Page 73: "the river passes Bohemian Grove": A classic and wildly entertaining source on the prolific lore surrounding Bohemian Grove is Philip Weiss, "Masters of the Universe Go to Camp: Inside the Bohemian Grove," *Spy Magazine* (November 1989), 58–76.

Page 76: "Then, as author and local resident Manjula Martin writes": Manjula Martin, *The Last Fire Season: A Personal and Pyronatural History* (New York: Pantheon, 2024), 20–21.

CHAPTER FIVE: A RECHARGED AQUIFER

Page 87: "*human giver*, a woman who is held": Kate Manne, *Down Girl: The Logic of Misogyny* (Oxford: Oxford University Press, 2018), 301.

Page 89: "Smith's husband introduces her": Maggie Smith, *You Could Make This Place Beautiful: A Memoir* (New York: One Signal Publishers, 2023), 60.

Page 90: "I nodded at Smith's frustration": Smith, *You Could Make This Place Beautiful*, 81.

Page 90: "The time women spend": See Arlie Hochschild, *The Second Shift: Working Families and the Revolution at Home* (New York: Penguin, 1989); Paula England, "The Gender Revolution: Uneven and Stalled," in *Gender & Society* 24, no. 149 (2010).

Page 90: "we see a period of rapid change": Alison Daminger, *What's on Her Mind: The Mental Workload of Family Life* (Princeton, NJ: Princeton University Press, 2025), 6. Daminger's fascinating and thorough work offers a brilliant exploration of the cognitive dimensions of household labor, as well as a wealth of further citations.

Page 91: "The women of my generation": Jessica Blough, "Women of My Generation Were Sold a Bill of Goods: Sarah Manguso on the Deception of Marriage," *Alta* (July 25, 2024), https://www.altaonline.com/dispatches/a61699800/women-of-my-generation-were-sold-a-bill-of-goods/.

Page 91: "the author Ada Calhoun writes": Ada Calhoun, "When 'Having It All' Becomes 'Wanting a Divorce,'" *TIME* (February 12, 2025), https://time.com/7216367/gen-x-women-midlife-divorce-essay/.

Page 91: "According to a 2015 study": "Women More Likely Than Men to Initiate Divorces, but Not Non-Marital Breakups," American Sociological Association, August 22, 2015, https://www.asanet.org/women-more-likely-men-initiate-divorces-not-non-marital-breakups/.

Page 92: "marriage in Victorian Britain": Some reform of divorce law was implemented in the 1850s, but marriage remained deeply unequal and full divorces allowing remarriage remained very difficult to obtain. See Philip Mallett, "Women and the Law in

Victorian England," in The Victorian City, 2025, https://victoriancity.wp.st-andrews.ac.uk/women-and-the-law-in-victorian-england/. While there are countless sources on the legal history of women and marriage, a lively and polemical overview of particularly misogynist legal history can be found in Lyz Lenz, *This American Ex-Wife: How I Ended My Marriage and Started My Life* (New York: Crown, 2024), especially chapter 3.

Page 92: "It is possible to have a happy and equal marriage": Lenz, *This American Ex-Wife*, 73.

Page 93: "as a woman in a society that pretends equality": Kate Hamilton, *Mad Wife: A Memoir* (Boston: Beacon Press, 2024), 110.

Page 94: "Even the ones who seemed to know we were doomed": Scaachi Koul, "When Couples Therapy Becomes a Weapon," *The Cut* (May 14, 2024), https://www.thecut.com/article/does-couples-therapy-work.html.

Page 95: "One of the sly reveals": Leslie Jamison, *Splinters: Another Kind of Love Story* (New York: Little Brown, 2024), 67.

Page 97: "Marriage . . . trains women to erase ourselves": Hamilton, *Mad Wife*, 110.

Page 99: "A patriarchal culture such as ours": Hamilton, *Mad Wife*, 6.

Page 99: "A husband might be nothing but": Sarah Manguso, *Liars: A Novel* (New York: Hogarth, 2024), 239.

Page 103: "A Black teenager, Joan Means Khabele": Hannah Uebele, "Honoring the Activist Who Sparked the Integration of Barton Springs," *Austin Chronicle* (April 15, 2022), https://www.austinchronicle.com/news/2022-04-15/honoring-the-activist-who-sparked-the-integration-of-barton-springs-pool/.

Page 103: "Khabele passed away": Luz Moreno-Lozano, "Austin Will Name Bathhouse After Woman Who Helped Desegregate Barton Springs Pool," KUT News (April 11, 2024), https://www.kut.org/austin/2024-04-11/joan-means-khabele-barton-springs-pool-bathhouse-austin-name.

Page 105: "there was in me an awful thing": Cheryl Strayed, *Tiny Beautiful Things: Advice on Love and Life from Dear Sugar* (New York: Vintage Books, 2012), 170–71.

Page 105: "continuously asking for permission": Kimberly Harrington, "Nothing Tastes as Good as Final Feels," *Honey Stay Super*, Substack (March 31, 2024), https://kimberlyharrington.substack.com/p/nothing-tastes-as-good-as-final-feels.

CHAPTER SIX: A TALE OF TWO WATERSHEDS

Page 110: "Cherokee, where a gold mine once boomed": "Cherokee, California," Western Mining History, https://westernmininghistory.com/towns/california/cherokee/.

Page 110: "by Cherokee men": Park Service, "Cherokee, Butte County," A History of American Indians in California: Historic Sites, https://www.nps.gov/parkhistory/online_books/5views/5views1h14.htm.

Page 116: "one of those special swimming holes": Timothy H. Joyce, *Swimming Holes of California*, 2nd ed. (n.p.: Sierra Publications, 2013), 71.

CHAPTER SEVEN: THE ENCHANTED LAKE

Page 134: "Payahuunadu, this country of flowing water": Kendra Atleework, *Miracle Country: A Memoir* (Chapel Hill, NC: Algonquin Books, 2020), 32.

CHAPTER EIGHT: ROCKS AND A HARD PLACE

Page 143: "in a picture book that transfixed me": Kit Williams, *Masquerade* (London: Jonathan Cape, 1979).

Page 144: "I've long relied on": See Timothy H. Joyce, *Swimming Holes of California* (n.p.: Sierra Publications, 2013), and *Swimming Holes of California: Pro Tour*, 2nd ed. (n.p.: Sierra Publications, 2018); Pancho Doll, *Day Trips with a Splash: Swimming Holes of California* (San Diego: Running Water Publications, 1997; revised edition, 2003); and Caroline Clements and Dillon Seitchik-Reardon,

Places We Swim California: The Best Beaches, Rock Pools, Waterfalls, Rivers, Gorges, Lakes, and Hot Springs (Melbourne: Hardie Grant Explore, 2024).

Page 146: "Aging does not have to be a dispiriting spiral": Caroline Paul, *Tough Broad: From Boogie Boarding to Wing Walking—How Outdoor Adventure Improves Our Lives as We Age* (New York: Bloomsbury, 2024), 37.

Page 147: "You're on an adventure when you're reaching": Paul, *Tough Broad*, 10.

Page 148: "Here's a swimming hole that discriminates": Doll, *Swimming Holes of California*, 77.

Page 153: "Favorite almond butter–banana snacking cake": For this and many other excellent recipes, see Yossi Arefi, *Snacking Cakes: Simple Treats for Anytime Cravings* (New York: Clarkson Potter, 2020), 87.

CHAPTER NINE: THE SALT SEA

Page 160: "I was like a poster child": See Alison Daminger, *What's on Her Mind: The Mental Workload of Family Life* (Princeton, NJ: Princeton University Press, 2025). See also the discussion of mental load and gendered labor in chapter 5.

Page 161: "I have often eaten an egg": M. F. K. Fisher, *An Alphabet for Gourmets*, in *The Art of Eating* (New York: Collier, 1990), 577.

Page 161: "I resolved to establish myself": Fisher, *An Alphabet for Gourmets*, 579.

Page 162: "When I became the restaurant critic": I wrote at more length about this incident and the pleasure and perils of a woman being alone; see Kate Washington, "It's Still Radical for a Woman to Be Alone," *Dame Magazine* (November 26, 2018), https://www.damemagazine.com/2018/11/26/its-still-radical-for-a-woman-to-be-alone/.

Page 172: "It took me several years": Fisher, *An Alphabet for Gourmets*, 579.

CHAPTER TEN: THE GOLDEN RIVER

Page 181: "In a year and a half, hydraulic mining": John McPhee, *Assembling California* (New York: Farrar, Straus & Giroux, 1993), 64.

Page 181: "Upriver, McPhee writes": McPhee, *Assembling California*, 43–44.

Page 181: "Judge Lorenzo Sawyer ruled": See "North Bloomfield Hydraulic Mining Case," an online highlight from the National Archives, at https://www.archives.gov/san-francisco/highlights/north-bloomfield. The original files are housed at the National Archives in San Francisco.

Page 181: "flushed-away ground": McPhee, *Assembling California*, 45.

AFTERWORD: ALL THE DUNKS AND BEYOND

Page 192: "Physician Mark Harper's *Chill*": Mark Harper, *Chill: The Cold Water Swim Cure* (San Francisco: Chronicle, 2022), suggests that a regular program of cold-water swimming can help with depression, chronic pain, surgery recovery, fibromyalgia, and much more, and cites many scientific papers and books that take a deeper look at the science behind his plan.

Page 193: "makes [her] feel alive": Katherine May, *Wintering: The Power of Rest and Retreat in Difficult Times* (New York: Riverhead, 2020), 190.